MONSTER POETRY

THE NORTH

Edited By Brixie Payne

First published in Great Britain in 2018 by:

Young Writers
Remus House
Coltsfoot Drive
Peterborough
PE2 9BF
Telephone: 01733 890066
Website: www.youngwriters.co.uk

All Rights Reserved
Book Design by Ben Reeves
© Copyright Contributors 2018
SB ISBN 978-1-78896-837-9
Printed and bound in the UK by BookPrintingUK
Website: www.bookprintinguk.com
YB0378HZ

FOREWORD

Young Writers was created in 1991 with the express purpose of promoting and encouraging creative writing. Each competition we create is tailored to the relevant age group, hopefully giving each child the inspiration and incentive to create their own piece of writing, whether it's a poem or a short story. We truly believe that seeing it in print gives pupils a sense of achievement and pride in their work and themselves.

Our latest competition, Monster Poetry, focuses on uncovering the different techniques used in poetry and encouraging pupils to explore new ways to write a poem. Using a mix of imagination, expression and poetic styles, this anthology is an impressive snapshot of the inventive, original and skilful writing of young people today. These poems showcase the creativity and talent of these budding new writers as they learn the skills of writing, and we hope you are as entertained by them as we are.

CONTENTS

Independent Entries

Aaditya Saini (6)	1
Monjola Opemiposi Guduza (6)	2

Ashurst Primary School, Blackbrook

Abbie Lohrenz (8)	3
Sophie Kenyon (8)	4
Amy Lloyd (8)	6
John Robie (8)	7
Emily Johnstone (8)	8

Greenleas Primary School, Wallasey

Ruby Lolley (10)	9
Darcey Murdoch-Hughes (9)	10
Daisy Isobel Thomas (10)	12
Charlotte Woods (10)	14
Alinka Stewart (10)	15
Katie Cooper (9)	16
Phoebe Ann Carroll (9)	17
Liam Murphy (10)	18
Eleanor Murphy (10)	19
Emme Foster-Hyde (9)	20
Hattie Spicer (9)	21
Isabelle Craggs (9)	22
Frankie Lucas Davies (10)	23

Gurney Pease Academy, Darlington

Naomi Matilda Kundu-Dunn (8)	24
Grace Williams (8)	25
April Mansfield (7)	26

Jack Emrys Parry (7)	27
Layla Blackett (8)	28
Ewan Gavin Mackenzie (8)	29
Joe James English (7)	30
Zak-Jay Ruston (8)	31
Libbi Wilson (8)	32
Daniel Peel (8)	33
Liam Atkinson (8)	34
Finley Leo Jenkinson (8)	35
Ethan Andrew Dixon (8)	36
Kian Rondina (8)	37

Junction Farm Primary School, Eaglescliffe

Isobel Kirton (10)	38
Jesse-David Ukemeabasi C Kwentoh (11)	39

Lakeside School, Liverpool

Jake Ellis (8)	40
Demi Murphy (8)	41
Charlie-Ann Bailey (9)	42

Larkfield Primary School, Southport

Sam Duffy (11)	43
Hollie Ann Taylor (11)	44
Matthew Michie (10)	46
Tom Robert Lee (11)	47
Sophie Askew (11)	48
Kate Duffy (11)	49
Freya Moorcroft-Jones (10)	50
Sarah Karymow (11)	51
Hannah Grundy (10)	52

Matthew Waddington (10)	53

Longmoor Community Primary School, Liverpool

Ella-Grace Hanson (9)	54
Isla Tattersall (10)	55
Ruby Sharp (9)	56

Merchant Taylors' Primary School, Liverpool

Amelie Katz-Brennan (8)	57
Elouise Hosey (9)	58
Lola Patel (9)	60
Gabriella Morrissey (9)	62
Verity Clark (9)	64
Evangeline Nesbitt McCrone (9)	66
Nekaa Arulanathan (9)	67
Mia Hanley (9)	68
Tia Patel (9)	70
Sofia Lienn Shakespeare (9)	72
Ava Schorah (9)	74
Anju Roy (9)	75
Mya Laycock (9)	76
Heather Marshall (9)	77
Dione Doctzan (9)	78
Harriet Munro (9)	79
Harriet Vernon (8)	80
Annabelle Mettrick (9)	82

Phoenix Primary School, Liverpool

Harry Wynne (10)	83
Cleo Mckenna (10)	84
Charlie Paul O'Hagan (10)	85
Aimee-Lee Doughtery (10)	86
Olivia Dolan (10)	87
Rhys Weir (10)	88

Plantation Primary School, Halewood

Jessica Service (8)	89
Sophie Houghton (10)	90

Robin Hood Primary School, Robin Hood

Gracie Florence Scollen (10)	91

St Francis De Sales Catholic Junior School, Liverpool

Daisy Lynch (7)	92
Daniel Middlehurst (10)	94
Caitlyn Carragher-Leigh (8)	96
Muhammad Aashir (10)	98
Emily Forshaw (10)	100
Lexie Bruns (9)	102
Joseph Collins (10)	104
Jasmine Young (9)	106
Tom Lynch (7)	108
Niamh Ferguson (8)	110
Sienna McCready (11)	112
Darren Herlihy (8)	114
Caitlin Louise Kelly (10)	115
Ruby O'Brien (8)	116
Oliver Smith (8)	117
Elizabeth Doherty (11)	118
Simra Nadim (10)	120
Kaysey Sherlock (11)	122
Anthony Muren (9)	123
Kaliah Nicholson (8)	124
Maisie-Jane Perry (9)	125
Lydia Katherine Quayle (7)	126
Holly Louise Williams (9)	128
Isabella Louise Blain (10)	130
Lilly May Dunning (11)	131
Lili Lou Tregunna (8)	132
Neve Garvey (8)	133
Krystal Natalie Sanders (9)	134
Robert Chadwick Jr (11)	135
Gabriella Calder (10)	136

Daniel Connor (7)	138
Keira Harrison (10)	139
Isobel Moran (10)	140
Layton James (8)	142
Harry Shallcross (9)	143
Lexi Saunderson (9)	144
Isabella May Bennett (11)	145
Harley James Whittingham (10)	146
Ella Harper (11)	147
Jessica Sheridan (11)	148
Milly-Ann McDermott (9)	149
Lizzie Cassin (8)	150
Thomas Morley-Healy (9)	151
Isabelle Louisa Edwards (10)	152
Rae Hynds (10)	153
Scarlett Conlan (7)	154
Alfie Walsh (9)	155

St Joseph's Washington RC School, Washington

Ava Roberts (9)	156
Katie Muir (9)	157
Eva Alexandra Smith (9)	158
Misia Ograbek (10)	159
Taylor Paul Jacklin (9)	160
Lennon Jay Liddle (9)	161
Katie Robinson (9)	162
Sonny Evin Liddle (9)	164
Alfie Joe Wilson (9)	165
Emily Richardson (9)	166

St Patrick's RC Primary School, Ryhope

Niall Bruce (8)	167
Hannah Naisbitt (9)	168
Zanyar Mohammed (9)	170
Hannah Neal (10)	172
Ruby Clark (9)	174
Theo Anthony Price (9)	175
Abrahim Ahmed Umar (9)	176
Millie Wake (10)	177
Nathan Jones (9)	178

Owen Hunt (10)	179
Jessica Hartnett (9)	180
Maha Fazal Umar (10)	181
Lilly Jane Sillett (9)	182
Daniel Baines (9)	183
Jensen Andrew Howe (9)	184
Harriet Westoe (9)	185
Jessica Lei Howe (9)	186
Maddie Stoodley (10)	187
Jack Slee (9)	188
Michael Henry Hackett (10)	189

Stoneferry Primary School, Hull

Chloe Grace Greenwood (9)	190

Three Lane Ends Academy, Castleford

Charlotte Olivia Hawkin (10)	191

Wargrave CE Primary School, Newton-Le-Willows

Keira Marshall (10)	193
Zahra Bhatti (9)	194
George Cain-Morris (9)	196
Lucy Lee (10)	198
Alyssa Pritchard (9)	200
Talia Grace Moorhouse (9)	202
Sophie Littler (9)	203
Francesca Hadaway (8)	204
Corbin Holmes (8)	205
Chloe Grace Edwards (8)	206
Aleisha Gorman (9)	208
Euan Stephen Arthur Adams (10)	209
Hayden Davis (10)	210
Erin Elyse Crossland (8)	211

THE POEMS

My Crescent Monster

You make me happy when I am sad,
You call me good when others call me bad,
You sleep with me at night in the dark,
You calm down my dog when it barks,
You help me with my studies, with games and everything,
You change my winter into spring,
You make me comfortable with your loving words,
I can't fly, you fly for me like a bird,
When I fall, your magic touch ends pain,
You bring me chocolate and candy canes,
To please me you turn in heavy rain,
We are always together like friends,
People call you Monster, I call you Crescent,
You entertain me with tricks when I feel bored,
You make me feel special when I am ignored,
People call you silly, scary and odd,
But you are the best gift given by God.

Aaditya Saini (6)

The Not Worry Monster

I love monsters, they never scare me,
Because I love to spin with them,
And march around with them,
They never scare me because I am friendly,
And they do not worry,
When I am sick,
They do not worry,
And when I shout at them,
They are quiet,
They always, always, always come when I am crying,
But they still don't worry.

Monjola Opemiposi Guduza (6)

A Terrifying Time For Bug-Eyed Bob

Bug-Eyed Bob,
Malicious as a minotaur,
As hairy as a hound,
Had a friend called Sharp-Toothed Sid,
Whose teeth could bite through a dustbin lid,
Off they went to the haunted house,
Got terrified by a miniscule mouse,
Bob let out a terrific trump,
It was so loud, it made Sid jump,
Then out of the wall, there came a ghost,
I don't know who it frightened the most,
Bob clutched his heart and dropped down dead,
"It's time for lunch," Sharp-Toothed Sid said,
And that's the end of the story,
Of another day on Planet Gory.

Abbie Lohrenz (8)
Ashurst Primary School, Blackbrook

The Magic Spell

A furry, spotty creature wandered in the wood,
He came across a stick lying on the ground,
"Mmm, what have I found?"
He decided to give it a wave around.

Bish! Bash! Boom!
Sparkles and lights shone,
He thought to himself, *what's going on?*
Suddenly it stopped and the furry creature was gone,
Nothing was left, apart from a slimy green frog and a wand.

The frog gave a big croak and was not happy at all,
From being big and furry, he was now green and small,
He needed that wand to change him back in a hurry,
But down flew a bird and picked it up with a scurry.

As he stood there and watched the wand disappear,
He heard lots of shouting and a great, big cheer,
"Hooray!" shouted the people,
"The scary monster can no longer give chase,
As now there is only a small, slimy frog in his place!"

Sophie Kenyon (8)
Ashurst Primary School, Blackbrook

Tiny Is Not Tiny

Tiny is huge, Tiny is colossal,
Older than me and you, older than a fossil,
Tiny has wings, Tiny can fly,
Like a big fat bumblebee soaring in the sky,
Tiny has a friend, Tiny has a pal,
And Shiny lives far away, near the shipping canal,
Tiny's like a rainbow, Tiny's like a cloud,
Fluffy on the outside and also very proud,
Tiny is gentle, Tiny is kind,
Tiny lives under my bed, but I don't mind,
Tiny is clever, Tiny likes to learn,
I've even caught her reading my book when it was my turn.

Amy Lloyd (8)
Ashurst Primary School, Blackbrook

The Aliens

I have an alien friend from a planet called Great Trinky,
He has an awful name, he's called Stinky,
He is very clever and can do his times tables,
He is funny and kind and likes to play with my mum's TV cables,
I'm sad whenever he goes back to his home, but...
My mum gets worried when he comes back,
And says, "Tut, tut, tut."

John Robie (8)
Ashurst Primary School, Blackbrook

Terrifying Town

I went to sleep,
As I do every night,
I saw a monster town,
There were green, pink, black and blue monsters,
They had scaly feet, there were all types,
But there was one in particular that I liked,
It had two terrible tails,
A handsome human body,
Horrendous hair,
And terrifying tentacles,
He shape-shifted before my eyes,
Into a green, slimy, sloppy, gooey mess,
Then he shape-shifted again,
Into a reeking, melting yellow thing.

Emily Johnstone (8)
Ashurst Primary School, Blackbrook

The Blood Sucker

An unpleasant thing came,
The malicious creature's eyes took aim,
It was wicked with a streak of coal-black hair,
Which for sure, I could not bear.

It had horrifying teeth as white as snow,
As it roamed, its cape would blow,
The monstrous thing was certainly a vampire,
Who, to be truly honest, wasn't a very good liar.

The towering thing was terrible,
He was something unacceptable,
His sadness spread,
As he turned his head.

When you heard the sound of a whistle,
You knew it wouldn't be a eucatastrophe.

Ruby Lolley (10)
Greenleas Primary School, Wallasey

Monster In The Wardrobe

There's a monster in the wardrobe,
You will see,
He's coming out to haunt us,
Yes, you and me!
He sees you when you're sleeping,
He knows when you're awake,
So don't go to bed too early, yes, don't make my mistake!

You see, I went to bed *too* early,
Because I was sleepy from my exam the day before,
To be exact, it was at, erm, twenty past four,
Oh yes, I remember now, I woke suddenly with a fright,
For a towering shadow crept up behind me, eyes glaring so bright.

His teeth were like chainsaws, a million, not a few,
His fur as black as night, oh, what a scary view!
I leapt up out of my bed, away from his long, sharp claws,
And paced down the stairs to escape his harmful jaws,

I peered around the corner, hoping for joy,
But what I saw was a tiny, evil beast with small, piercing claws.

I raced back up the stairs,
I thought, *what a week!*
I leapt into my bed saying, "Mummy, I've seen a freak!"
She came and sat down and said, "Deary, what's the matter?"
"Oh Mummy, it's a monster, it is trying to batter..."
"Batter what? A cake?" Mum said,
"Oh, that's silly, I think it's in your head."

But I think she might've been right, because all that now lies on my bed,
Is a tiny toy monster left, lying dead!

Darcey Murdoch-Hughes (9)
Greenleas Primary School, Wallasey

Bibble The Monster

Bibble was the kindest monster,
He was woolly, hairy and like a fairy,
He lived in the fiery land of Zaploo,
Which might sound kind of scary,
The planet was full of volcanoes and other stuff,
But underneath the surface, it was really full of love.

But to the north of that fiery world,
Past the galaxy called Siron,
Was the dark and mysterious Planet Erk ruled by the evil king Biron,
Biron had a thousand eyes, he could see everywhere,
He could make the bravest tremble with fear under his nightmare glare.

Another miserable day passed on Planet Erk,
People never got to play as all they did was work,
They didn't know how to love or laugh with anyone,
All the grumpy monsters never had any fun,
But what they didn't know was that soon they all would.

When Bibble found out about all the misery,
He rushed right over to Planet Erk to fill their hearts with glee,
The evil king Biron sat on his throne,
The evil king Biron attacked poor Bibble,
And then started to push and shove,
But with his thousand eyes, Biron couldn't help but see Bibble's love.

"I'll change my ways!" the king declared,
Freeing all his people,
They laughed and danced with love and joy,
Every girl and every boy.

Daisy Isobel Thomas (10)
Greenleas Primary School, Wallasey

Have You Ever Touched Fire?

Fire was born on a star,
Its fiesty attitude made its fur burn,
Its fur was like fire,
With red, yellow and orange fur,
Its brown eyes sparkled when it got mad,
For years it had been living on a star,
But then, suddenly, there was a meteor crash,
So all of the little monsters,
Were forced down to Earth with a big bash,
But Fire didn't want to go,
So as it got mad, fire came from it,
They were saved once again,
Everyone cheered and shouted, "Whoa!"

Charlotte Woods (10)
Greenleas Primary School, Wallasey

The Monster From Mars

It was the middle of the night, no one was awake,
I was fast asleep but then my bed began to shake,
There was a rumble under the bed,
I took a look and saw eyes that were red,
It came out and showed itself,
It was as large as a giant,
It had razor-sharp horns and three red eyes,
"My name's Googley," he said with a smile,
His breath was a wave of sickness,
His fur was covered in mould,
He whispered to me and asked me if I was cold,
I shivered but replied, "Yes," with a grin on my face,
He gave me a cuddle, there wasn't much space,
I asked, "Where are you from?"
He said back to me, "I come from Mars."

Alinka Stewart (10)
Greenleas Primary School, Wallasey

The Slicer In The Shadows

She was there, hiding in the shadows,
Waiting, lonely, without a friend,
She was gentle really,
But her fangs looked scary,
So she sat in the bush all alone.

"I'll have no friends," she sighed in the shadows,
"I'm Slicer so I'll try to stay strong."
Alone in the bush she crouched,
A peep had come from behind her,
Surely it had come from behind her!

And there behind her, in the shadows,
A little thing was crouching,
And she looked exactly like her,
She was nearly her twin sister,
And finally, a friend she could have!

Katie Cooper (9)
Greenleas Primary School, Wallasey

The Forever Lost Creature

There once was a creature,
Who lived on Mars,
He loved to eat stars,
His name was Wars.

He once travelled to Earth on a rocket,
He saw shooting stars,
From Earth to Mars,
He ate some stars.

In a rocket he cooked,
Poison, poison, poison,
He ate it and died!

Phoebe Ann Carroll (9)
Greenleas Primary School, Wallasey

Fluff Monster

Here comes the fluffy ball know as Fluff,
But underneath that furry fur,
Is something quite rough,
She is always crazy,
The opposite of lazy,
She eats with her hands,
Not like a lady,
Even though she is sixteen,
She acts like a kid,
But you just won't believe what she did,
She set fire to the ocean,
She made a mad science lab,
And drank an invisibility potion,
You're lucky she moved to India,
To live with her aunt Pew,
But if you'd lived with her before,
The words you'd be saying would be few.

Liam Murphy (10)
Greenleas Primary School, Wallasey

Monster And The Maze

Say hello if you dare,
He will eat your skin and your hair,
Some people might think he's good,
But the evil monster will drink your blood,
He will creep up on you in the night,
And give you such a scary fright,
If you go into the maze,
It will be the end of your days,
Take this warning in your stride,
The others didn't and they all died.

Eleanor Murphy (10)
Greenleas Primary School, Wallasey

Fegul

Deadly,
This monster can kill with one bite,
Its horns are filled with deadly venom,
Its eyes are as red as blood,
Fangs, blood is dripping from its fangs,
Four arms, four legs, twenty fingers, twenty toes,
Claws that can rip through anything,
Small as a turtle, it eats people for food,
It's left space to destroy Earth...

Emme Foster-Hyde (9)
Greenleas Primary School, Wallasey

Bloodthirsty Mermaid

There is a monster called Diana,
She lives in the sea far, far away,
She is scaly, threatening and ugly,
And she lives by the bay,
She eats flesh,
She is cruel and murderous,
She drowns and she kills,
And she is horrendous,
Do not dare ask for mercy,
Because she is so bloodthirsty.

Hattie Spicer (9)
Greenleas Primary School, Wallasey

The Kind Sea Monster

Sandy is a mermaid who is very green,
She does not like to be seen.

Sandy is very kind,
And lots of seashells she likes to find.

Sometimes she is a seagull and looks down at the high seas,
When she is up in the sky, she flies with the breeze.

Isabelle Craggs (9)
Greenleas Primary School, Wallasey

Fire Trapper

Deep in the Antarctic Sea, under the ice,
Lives a furry glow, never burning out,
With the tail of a fish,
And the head of a croc,
And fire on its back,
And dragon eyes that glow in the night,
As it swims through the deep, frozen sea,
Things in its sight will get a fright,
In one single bite.

Frankie Lucas Davies (10)
Greenleas Primary School, Wallasey

The Silliest Monster Ever

There lived a furry pink monster whose name was Silly Billy,
Her hair was the colour of strawberry ice cream,
She had eighty eyes,
She had seventy-nine tiny eyes and one massive middle eye,
If you got too close to her you could die,
She had four different types of legs,
Because she was silly, she was called Silly Billy,
All the other monster's eyes were colourful,
Her face was the colour of a pink rose,
She had no nose,
Her nails were as sharp as a piece of glass,
She came from the moon,
And all she wanted was a friend.

Naomi Matilda Kundu-Dunn (8)
Gurney Pease Academy, Darlington

The Red, Green And Horrible Monster

There lived a creepy monster,
Whose name was Greeny,
His eyes were the colour of the Devil's blood,
He had two mouths and nineteen eyes that were blue,
His face was the colour of grass,
His arms and freckles were on his big body,
Like a frog, he ate flies,
His teeth were as sharp as a knife,
His spots were as big as the moon,
His teeth were the colour of a lemon,
He had a razor-sharp smile,
He liked to drink blood,
And would eat you all at once,
He had twelve fangs altogether.

Grace Williams (8)
Gurney Pease Academy, Darlington

Child Thieving Monster

There lived a child chewing monster,
Whose name was Blood-Cruncher,
Her mouth was the colour of lava,
She had the letter M for her eyebrows,
They showed she liked McDonald's,
And her tentacles were the colour of the sea at night,
Her tentacles and body were purple and bright,
They were like the sun setting,
Her claws were as dark as the night,
Her teeth were covered in so much blood,
With a touch of black for the scariest scream,
She was a screaming monster.

April Mansfield (7)
Gurney Pease Academy, Darlington

Bobby Bell

There lived a humongous monster,
Whose name was Bobby,
His eyes were the colour of a green swamp,
He had a brown body and purple bogies in his nose,
And a red face the colour of tomato ketchup,
His feet were very strong and big,
Like a dinosaur or King Kong,
His neck was the smallest one ever!
His hair was as spiky as a cactus,
His tongue was the colour of bubblegum ice cream,
And he would make you scream,
Argh!

Jack Emrys Parry (7)
Gurney Pease Academy, Darlington

Spiky's Star Monster Poem

There lived a spiky star monster whose name was Spiky,
Her eyes were the colour of a rose,
She loved to pose,
She had eight spikes on her feet and four legs,
And a blue face the colour of the sky,
Her skin and eyes were oh-so dull like the night,
Her body was as spiky as a hedgehog,
Her legs were as long as a giraffe,
Her eyes were yellow like bananas,
Her teeth were the colour of apples,
She had a spiky front tooth.

Layla Blackett (8)
Gurney Pease Academy, Darlington

MONSTER POETRY - THE NORTH

The Dark Dream

There lived an ugly devil,
Whose name was Worm Eater,
His leg was the colour of rotten cheese,
He had spots on his nose like green peas,
And a neck the colour of mud!
His fingers and feet were wrinkly and thick,
Like an old tortoise with a walking stick,
His breath was as smelly as football socks,
His tooth was as blue as the sea,
His back was as tall as a waterfall,
With a prickly tail as red as a rose.

Ewan Gavin Mackenzie (8)
Gurney Pease Academy, Darlington

The Selfish Monster Spotty

There lived a funny monster,
Whose name was Spotty,
His eyes were the colour of the Devil,
He had a fiery and spotty body,
And his ears were the colour of grapes,
His legs and hair were as orange as spaghetti,
He was like an orange fireball,
His legs were as blue as the sky,
His spots were as yellow as a banana,
His hair was the colour of soil in the deep ground with worms that could eat you!

Joe James English (7)
Gurney Pease Academy, Darlington

Jimbob

There lived a friendly monster called Jimbob,
His ear was the colour of a turtle's body,
He had two blue and two black teeth,
And an eye the colour of beef,
His tail and legs were very long,
Like a swamp with a big pong,
His ear was as small as a pumpkin pie,
His legs were as blue as the sky,
His mouth was the colour of the deep blue sea,
And he liked to eat tuna fish for his tea.

Zak-Jay Ruston (8)
Gurney Pease Academy, Darlington

Marry B The Monster

There lived a horrifying monster,
Whose name was Marry B,
Her face was the colour of brown tea,
She had eight green, sparkling eyes,
And a red and white Santa hat,
And a diamond the colour of the sky,
Her strong legs and powerful feet,
Could stomp through the forest like an angry gorilla,
Her stinger was as sharp as a knife,
Her hair was the colour peach with a sprinkle of green.

Libbi Wilson (8)
Gurney Pease Academy, Darlington

Zack The Monster

There lived a cute monster called Zack,
His eyes were the colour of caramel,
He had a dash of brown and lashings of yellow on his body,
And a mouth the colour of the Devil,
His body was a slimeball,
His nose and hair were nowhere to be seen,
His mouth was a fireball,
His body was a pile of dirt,
When you hit him, it hurt,
His body was the colour of a smelly swamp.

Daniel Peel (8)
Gurney Pease Academy, Darlington

Pikachu

There lived a horrible monster,
Whose name was Pikachu,
His eyes were the colour of the sun,
He had ten tongues and two eyes,
His tail and nose were pea-green,
Like a swampy jelly in the bath,
His teeth were black,
His diamond was as black as mud,
His cheeks were the colour of blackberries,
With a brown mouth and swampy hair.

Liam Atkinson (8)
Gurney Pease Academy, Darlington

Chick Bee The Friendly Monster

There lived a friendly monster,
Whose name was Chick Bee,
His eyes were the colour of the Devil,
He had green pants and pink skin,
And a mouth the colour of red lava,
His tongue and teeth were as sharp as a shiny sword,
His eyelashes were as long as spider's legs,
His body was the colour of candyfloss with a peppermint stick.

Finley Leo Jenkinson (8)
Gurney Pease Academy, Darlington

Ethan The Monster

There lived a friendly monster whose name was Ethan,
He had green, blue and yellow legs,
And an eye the colour of lava,
His body and arms were bright yellow like the sun,
He ran as fast as a cheetah,
And he liked pepperoni pizza,
Ethan was a superhero monster,
Ethan's cape was as red as fire.

Ethan Andrew Dixon (8)
Gurney Pease Academy, Darlington

Beth The Monster

There lived a hairy monster,
Whose name was Beth,
Beth was powerful and moved quickly,
Her lips were the colour of lava,
She had green legs and yellow skin like a snake,
And an arm the colour of a lemon,
Her eyelashes and body were grey and yellow like the sun.

Kian Rondina (8)
Gurney Pease Academy, Darlington

Jim The Hero

Jim was loved by all,
Long, short, thin and tall,
But suddenly one day,
A dragon came his way,
Jim picked up a sword,
That belonged to the Lord,
He lifted it up in the sky,
Jim wanted to try,
He wanted to kill the dragon once and for all,
And so he did,
Jim was once zero,
But now he was a hero!

Isobel Kirton (10)
Junction Farm Primary School, Eaglescliffe

The Red Eye

Lurks in the darkest corners,
With the other multicoloured stalkers,
The opposite of positive,
Always dabbling in the negative,
Wanting you to come down,
Never wanting you to rise or wear a crown,
Switching into different colours,
Always has been evil.

Jesse-David Ukemeabasi C Kwentoh (11)
Junction Farm Primary School, Eaglescliffe

Conker Honker's Big Escape!

He stole from the rich and even the poor,
His skin could camouflage to avoid any war,
Naughty Conker and his two henchmen,
Lived under my school in their underwater den,
I heard them whispering and making a plan,
I thought I'd better act fast and call Superman,
Superman landed with a gigantic crash,
Quickly followed by his friend Flash,
They tried to catch Conker but he gave them a rash,
So they caught his henchmen and gave them a thrash!
Beaten and broken, tied to the top of a crane,
Conner Conker flew up high, never to be seen again...

Jake Ellis (8)
Lakeside School, Liverpool

MONSTER POETRY - THE NORTH

Smelly Ellie's Island Picnic

A baby monster called Smelly Ellie,
Was bored and sitting watching the telly,
A dark, stinky cave was her home,
She sat there all alone.

An invitation she did write,
To arrange a picnic the following night,
It was to be on an island nearby,
Where Kind Kai, Happy Harry and Ellie would fly!

Night-time came that following day,
Off they went to the island far away,
On it was a waterfall where they played all day,
The birds and quacking ducks sang a little song.

They sat by the lake and snaffled their food,
They had sandwiches and coffee that tasted really good,
The lovely sand between their toes put them in a gorgeous mood.

Demi Murphy (8)
Lakeside School, Liverpool

Billy And Lilly

There once were monsters called Billy and Lilly,
Who had two heads that looked rather silly,
He was as big as a house,
She was as quiet as a mouse,
And they lived in a land that was hilly.

Charlie-Ann Bailey (9)
Lakeside School, Liverpool

MONSTER POETRY - THE NORTH

The Tale Of The Lepri-Corn

The Lepri-Corn is very magical,
He is five foot two so he's kind of small,
People think that he is funny,
His best friend is a bunny.

The rabbit is white,
He stays up late at night,
So it's easy to give him a fright.

They once went to a magic show,
There were a few free seats in the front row,
They sat down with their snacks,
There was a magician with a magic hat.

He pulled a bunny out of his hat,
It was the bunny's brother named Matt,
They both opened their mouths in shock,
They wanted the show to come to a stop.

Sam Duffy (11)
Larkfield Primary School, Southport

Midget Mini

I was walking down the alley,
Wearing my school clothes and tie,
And then all of a sudden,
Something caught my eye.

It was in the bushes,
I did not make a sound,
I was scared, I was frightened,
A little monster had been roused.

He glanced at me,
He looked afraid,
He needed a home,
Or a place to stay.

I took him in my arms,
And held him tight,
He could come home with me,
And stay for the night.

Morning then came,
And the monster looked at me and said,

"I need to go home now,
Back to my bed."

I took him outside,
To where his mum and dad were,
Their ship was ready to go,
Up, up it would blow.

Remember, little monster,
Even though we're apart,
No matter where you are,
You'll always be in my heart.

Hollie Ann Taylor (11)
Larkfield Primary School, Southport

Bananademon

We were out for a run,
You will never guess what,
We saw something strange,
And then my life had to change,
It stared into my eyes,
And gave me a surprise,
We were only out to train,
But the Bananademon came,
It chased us back home,
And showed up in the dark,
Peeling the tree's bark,
We found him lurking in the hall,
But then a kid who was very tall,
Started a brawl,
The Bananademon vanished,
And the Bananademon was no more.

Matthew Michie (10)
Larkfield Primary School, Southport

Phil The Flying Robber Monster

Phil the flying robber monster flew across the land,
His friend Rob had a magic hand,
Once they went to a shop,
In a flash, they saw a cop.

They nicked some chips and ran off,
They went to the park and started to scoff,
But little did they know, they were being watched,
Suddenly, they were being chased by the cops.

After a few minutes, they were captured,
Their noses were fractured,
They were tortured in an electric chair,
Then they floated up into the air.

Tom Robert Lee (11)
Larkfield Primary School, Southport

The Fuzzy-Eyed Monster's Great Mistake

The fuzzy-eyed monster walked through the park,
To find in the pond a very scary shark.

The fuzzy-eyed monster jumped to his feet,
To find that he was already asleep.

Oh no, he thought, *not again!*
Had he really hidden in his den?

The shark said, "Hey you are late,
You were meant to take me on a play date!"

The fuzzy-eyed monster said, "Sorry mate,
I will see you tomorrow, here at eight!"

Sophie Askew (11)
Larkfield Primary School, Southport

The Uni-Doggy

On my travels around the world,
I've encountered many beasts,
But only one has stood out,
Let me go into deets,
Fur so soft,
Horn so light,
Eyes blue,
Collar bright,
Sounds like a dog,
Feels like silk,
Eyes like crystals,
Likes to drink milk,
A traveller,
Like me,
Very smart,
Called the Uni-Doggy.

Kate Duffy (11)
Larkfield Primary School, Southport

Monster In My Closet!

There's something in my closet,
I think I've really lost it,
It rumbles and it mumbles,
"Ah, those ghastly shoes!"

I don't know what to do,
I think it ate my shoe!
Oh no! Not my socks!

It needs to go now,
It hates my cat's miaow,
Go in kitty, good girl now,
Ciao!

Freya Moorcroft-Jones (10)
Larkfield Primary School, Southport

What Is It?

It is lurking in the forest,
I know it is trying to hide,
I find it eating porridge,
To it, it is just divine,
Its fur is thick and fluffy,
Its secret is lemon and lime,
Sometimes it gets puffy,
Now I know why it cries,
It is lurking in the forest,
It is a...
Butterfly yeti!

Sarah Karymow (11)
Larkfield Primary School, Southport

The Scissors

Scissors lives under my bed,
He is as mean as can be said,
He wants to live in a shed.

Scissors is green and likes to tease,
He likes to cut my hair,
It is not fair.

Scissors is mean,
It might seem,
But all he wants is a friend!

Hannah Grundy (10)
Larkfield Primary School, Southport

My Friend Is A Monster

My friend is a monster,
He is under my bed,
He comes out at night,
And gives me a fright,
He isn't a bad monster,
Just a bit scary,
And very hairy,
I am proud to have him as a friend,
My friend is a monster.

Matthew Waddington (10)
Larkfield Primary School, Southport

The Monster Register

Where's Jo? Finding a bow,
Where's Jude? Being rude.
Where's Josh? With the boss,
Where's Nancy? Being fancy.
Where's Megan? She's begging,
Where's Rosie? She's being nosy.
Where's Ella? With Bella,
Where's Molly? Finding her dolly.
Where's Poppy? Making a coffee,
Where's Faye? At the bay.
Where's Amy? With Jamie,
Where's Christopher? Getting the vinegar.
Where's Hayden? He's willing to trade,
Where's Victoria? With Gloria.
Where's Mia? She's got an idea,
Where's Bella? With some fella.
Where are all of the monsters?
They are meeting to eat lobsters.

Ella-Grace Hanson (9)
Longmoor Community Primary School, Liverpool

My Fluffy Friend

I have a fluffy friend,
Who drives me round the bend,
In the morning, she wakes up early,
But I can't get up, no really!
At lunch, she eats my food,
Which is very, very rude,
With my friends I like to play,
But she robs my best friend Esme,
At tea she eats some chips,
With ketchup on her lips,
At bath time she uses Matey,
She's been using too much lately,
At night she reads my story,
And snores as she sleeps,
But she snuggles up to me,
And that is very comfy,
I will love my fluffy friend,
Until the very, very end!

Isla Tattersall (10)
Longmoor Community Primary School, Liverpool

Is It Real?

Is it real?
Is it true?
Am I right?
Or are you?
Is it there?
In my hair?
Or is it stuck in my pear?
Can you hear it in my sock?
Can you see it turning the lock?
Is it blue like my eyes?
Or is it bigger than a cherry pie?
Has it got crooked teeth?
Or is it green like a leaf?
Has it got messy hair?
Or is it solid like a chair?
Has it got friends on Planet Blot?
Or has it been left alone to rot?
Hmm, I wonder, is it real or is it not?

Ruby Sharp (9)
Longmoor Community Primary School, Liverpool

Felicity's Fright

Fluffy, friendly and extremely funny,
Felicity the monster is one happy bunny,
She has saved up enough pocket money,
So she can travel to Iceland to visit her granny.

The day has come, she packs her bag,
A little worried about jet lag,
But oh no, she hits a snag,
She cannot find her Iceland flag.

Remembering a video she once watched on YouTube,
She taps her horn twice on an ice cube,
Off she goes at the speed of light,
Though giving herself a bit of a fright.

It really is such a breeze,
But she finds herself in a deep freeze,
Then she sees a light in the distance glowing,
She reaches out to tap the light with her horn...
It was just a dream, it is early morn.

Amelie Katz-Brennan (8)
Merchant Taylors' Primary School, Liverpool

Happy Not The Clown Monster

It was such a long time ago, people have forgotten,
That there was once a monster clown called Happy Not,
He was a clown with a happy face upside down,
Yes that's right, he had a frown.

He was scary, hairy and quite contrary,
And he didn't look like a fairy,
I assure you this story is true,
If you don't believe me then I will sue.

The circus wouldn't let him appear in the show,
They told him he was no good and had to go,
So he decided to get his own back,
"I will teach them to give me the sack!"

He scared all the other clowns away,
A circus without a clown would not last a day,

He was right and the audience numbers were down,
They cried, "This is no circus if there isn't a clown!"

As the crowd called for the clown to appear, there was a big flash,
And there he stood, scary, bright and brash,
He ran around, throwing custard pies in the faces of all about,
Causing them to scream and cry out.

When they cleaned themselves up and wiped themselves down,
They looked at each other and saw the face of a clown with a frown,
Then there were many clowns in many places,
With scary make-up all over their faces.

Elouise Hosey (9)
Merchant Taylors' Primary School, Liverpool

The People's Monster

I was born on Mars, millions of miles away,
Where no human can ever reach,
I'm good but I'm as cheeky as a monkey,
And as fluffy as a bunny,
But sometimes I can get very smelly!

I have four antennae in total,
One long and three short,
My antennae are so special and wonderful,
Because I can detect lonely people,
Who live on Planet Earth.

On Planet Earth, I live in an alley,
Which is as deep as the ocean,
And as dark as the night sky,
But I'm as shy as a kid in a new school.

Every now and then, my antennae vibrate,
They're like bumblebees when I sense a lonely person,
So I move out of my alley,
Like a floating candle.

I tap my lonely friend on the shoulder,
And I give them a big friendly smile,
And a big hug like a bear,
We then skip to the beach and build sandcastles,
We play in the sea and have ice cream until our bellies are full.

My lonely friend is then not lonely anymore,
They are as warm as the sun and as safe as a house,
Then I return home and go to sleep,
Feeling warm and knowing that I'm known,
As the People's Monster.

Lola Patel (9)
Merchant Taylors' Primary School, Liverpool

Timid Tabitha

Timid Tabitha lived all alone in a dark, gloomy cave,
Her guts were tangled and her skin was rough and spiky,
Nobody would give her a wave,
Her neck was coiled like a spring.

She had four stubby legs and three toes,
Fire would blast from her mouth,
She had a very strange-looking nose,
She longed for a friend because she was so lonely.

One day, she was very brave and came out of her habitat,
Although she was very frightened,
Tabitha really wanted to have a chat,
Her heart was filled with love and joy.

She spotted a little girl who appeared quite shy,
They looked at each other in surprise,
Then she approached her and said, "Hi!"
Tabitha then said hi back.

They played games in the sun,
Because the little girl and Tabitha had become best friends,
They had so much fun,
Tabitha wasn't lonely or sad!

Gabriella Morrissey (9)
Merchant Taylors' Primary School, Liverpool

My Mistake

He's big, he's strong,
He's no pet 'cause he's mean,
And if you ever see this guy,
You'll wish you'd never met,
For he has eyes as bright as the sun,
They can kill faster than a gun.

His stomach is round,
It's a great, hairy mound!
His ears are big and hairy,
And make him even more scary!

You wouldn't want to meet this guy,
If you were in an alley,
He would thrash you,
Like Andy Murray in a rally!

He's here,
Now he's there,
He zooms around everywhere!
And what he eats is...
You!

Oops, he's the complete opposite!
Sorry, my mistake!
Verity Clark (9)
Merchant Taylors' Primary School, Liverpool

Intergalactic Friends

Hi, my name is Jelot,
I come from the planet Goblelot,
From dusk until dawn, I travelled far,
Across the black night sky like a shooting star,
I flew to Earth in my spaceship,
In search of friendship,
It can be quite difficult when you look like me,
But it is past my looks you have to see,
For with my slimy octopus arms and my big pointy ears,
I tend to cause lots of fears,
But once you get to know me,
You will find that I'm full of glee,
I like to hover in the sky,
People wonder how something so big can fly,
I made two friends, the best you can get,
Now I need to go home, Chloe and Sophie I will not forget,
They would like to come back with me,
But their parents won't want them to miss their tea.

Evangeline Nesbitt McCrone (9)
Merchant Taylors' Primary School, Liverpool

The Loner

Do you dare seek me?
For I do try to hide,
I come from a galaxy far and wide,
Do you feel normal or do you feel old?
For I am left alone in a dump to rot,
I am a monstrous silhouette in the darkness,
Have you got friends, a family and a real home?
For I don't have friends, a family or a home,
I am a crucified silhouette, alone in the darkness,
Have you got used to living on Earth?
For I have never got a taste for it,
I am a tortured silhouette alone in the darkness,
Do you feel unique or do you feel the same?
I don't feel the English language flow in me,
For I am half human and half devil.

Nekaa Arulanathan (9)
Merchant Taylors' Primary School, Liverpool

Mozzie The Monster

Every night, Lizzie gets ready for bed,
With worries and woes still in her head,
The lights go off and bedtime returns,
Then comes Mozzie with eyes that burn,
The shape-shifting fiend growls with a bark,
Lizzie tries to be brave, alone in the dark,
Her eyes tight shut, but her imagination is awake,
Mozzie the monster, could she be...
As big as a house,
As small as a mouse,
Horribly hairy,
Very scary,
As large as a whale,
With a long, wide tail?
How she appears, you'll never know,
Because in Lizzie's imagination, you'll never go,
The door opens with a creak,
Tiptoeing in her room, Lizzie's mum tries to sneak,
A kiss on her cheek, her blanket tucked in,
Her fears fade way, all is good again,
Mozzie's burning eyes change to a familiar, friendly face,

Mozzie's hairy body now seems cute and cuddly,
There's not a sound for Lizzie to make,
Her teddy appears in the dark, she's no longer awake.

Mia Hanley (9)
Merchant Taylors' Primary School, Liverpool

Eco-Scare

For those who aren't eco-aware,
I slowly prowl, waiting to scare.
With my bushy green hair and long, grassy arms,
I camouflage until my eco-sensor alarms.

I appear from the shadows ready to pounce,
With my eco-message to loudly announce,
"Do not litter and recycle plastic.
Think of our planet and keep it fantastic."

When anyone meets me, they get a fright.
I'm always patrolling, day and night.
As I hide in the parks under the trees,
I admire my friends, the butterflies and bees.

The colours flying past against the sky so blue,
With busy honey-makers visiting flowers covered in dew.
I dream of a day when our planet is green,
When our waters are clear and the earth is clean.

I see the light in our new generation,
With young eco-teams that are spreading green education.

One day I shall no longer be needed as my job will be done,
I'll return to my rainforest and relax in the sun.

Tia Patel (9)
Merchant Taylors' Primary School, Liverpool

The Ghosticorn

There once was a creature,
That you would dream about in your dreams,
Its name was the Ghosticorn,
The Ghosticorn approached Planet Earth,
And I saw something in the sky.

I couldn't believe what I saw,
No wonder it was named the Ghosticorn,
Because it had a horn and was a ghost with wings,
It was multicoloured and had hooves.

I rushed outside and people were running away,
Then, suddenly, I saw it close up,
It was slimy, furry and cute,
I wondered why people were running away.

I was the only one left in the village,
So I took it with me,
So it could find somewhere to hide.

The next morning, everyone loved the mysterious creature,
Because I proved that it was not scary,

But the big question was,
Where did it come from?

Sofia Lienn Shakespeare (9)
Merchant Taylors' Primary School, Liverpool

What Is It?

Is it an alien?
But it's not slimy,
Is it a bird?
It's got wings,
Is it a cockroach?
But it's in the water,
Is it a dragon?
It has got scales,
Is it an elephant?
But it hasn't got a trunk,
Is it a frog?
It has a bit of green,
Is it a gargoyle?
But it's not made of stone,
Is it a horse?
It looks like one,
It's a...

Ava Schorah (9)
Merchant Taylors' Primary School, Liverpool

Voltron The Winged Beast!

I looked closely at the flying horror!
It was heading for Planet Earth!
Its name was Voltron and it had fangs as big as the Empire State!
It ate rotten eggs from the bin,
That's why its breath smelt revolting, nasty and repulsive,
It was as furry as a lamb,
But no one knew that it was a shape-shifter,
It could turn into anything!
Its tongue was yellow,
And its eyes were red,
Its mouth was dark and wide like a cave,
One day I met him under my bed,
When the day was dim...

Anju Roy (9)
Merchant Taylors' Primary School, Liverpool

Monster Monster

His name is Jack,
He lives in a sack,
Monster, monster, monster,
As red as a lobster,
He has four eyes,
He loves eating pies,
Monster, monster, monster,
As red as a lobster,
He is very, very hairy,
But not very scary,
Monster, monster, monster,
As red as a lobster,
He has sharp, pointy claws,
And giant jaws,
Monster, monster, monster,
As red as a lobster.

Mya Laycock (9)
Merchant Taylors' Primary School, Liverpool

You Can Call Me Fluff

I roll into every corner of this already filthy house,
I am minuscule,
No one knows how I have come to be here,
But they call me Fluff,
I am not just that, you know,
For I am magical and can make more of me,
I have one small eye and one big eye,
I have a moustache and I am fluffy,
I drift like a ghost everywhere,
I have horns and a tuft of hair,
But my magic comes from my unicorn horn,
And I am called Evil Fluff!

Heather Marshall (9)
Merchant Taylors' Primary School, Liverpool

It's Only A Dream, Child

Children, close your eyes,
And when I say, "Open!"
You can open your eyes,
Imagine this monster you soon will see,
Has four legs and giant knees,
It holds in its razor-sharp claws,
Three cards as big as oak trees,
It has big, hard, muscular arms,
Don't think that this monster won't harm,
It will tear you to pieces,
Its favourite food is from McDonald's,
It's children that it eats...
Child McNuggets,
So children, don't eat at McDonald's!
Open your eyes children,
You're dreaming, this is not true,
Oopsy-daisy, I forgot to tell you!

Dione Doctzan (9)
Merchant Taylors' Primary School, Liverpool

All About The Strange Scadazzle!

Scadazzle is a rainbow sneezing monster,
You'd better be cautious because he makes you nauseous,
With his rainbow fur and his brown fairy hair,
If you touch his toe, he will sneeze a magical rainbow,
He has lived in a shoe since the age of two,
He eats rocks and stones, they help grow his bones,
He walks with a giggle, a wiggle and a wriggle,
He dances happily until the sun sets, the stars shimmer,
And the moon shines bright in the magical night.

Harriet Munro (9)
Merchant Taylors' Primary School, Liverpool

My Goofy Green Monster

My goofy green monster,
Hides under my bed,
He gives me a fright,
When he jumps on my head.

My goofy green monster,
Is very cheeky,
He feels very hairy,
And is a little bit scary.

My goofy green monster,
Is as small as a mouse,
He's as hairy as a yeti,
But as playful as a louse.

My goofy green monster,
Is called Fred,
He's a silly billy,
With a very big head.

I love my goofy green monster,
He's fun,

Each night we play,
Until it turns to day.

Harriet Vernon (8)
Merchant Taylors' Primary School, Liverpool

My Monster

My monster is a rainbow-coloured monster,
She comes from Planet Zeg,
She has one enormous eye in the centre of her face,
My monster has smooth horns on the tip of her gigantic head,
She has a small, stripy body,
She can transform into any animal in the universe,
My monster lives outside in my tree house,
Only I know about my monster.

Annabelle Mettrick (9)
Merchant Taylors' Primary School, Liverpool

Zabeggra

His name is Zabeggra,
His hobby is feeding zebras,
He goes down mines,
He can blink many times,
His size is six feet six inches,
He never allows pinches,
He's afraid of the dark,
And also takes people apart,
He loves ice cream and cones,
And also has chocolate toes,
He's the friendliest monster yeti,
But don't get too close and don't be so keen,
He's the tickliest monster the world's ever seen,
Inside his house, in his basement, is a tickling machine,
It shows how many people he's tickled,
Each day he tickles ten people.

Harry Wynne (10)
Phoenix Primary School, Liverpool

Up, Up And Away

This is Fuzzy Wuzzy,
He lives in the clouds all alone,
One day he fell from his home,
But luckily enough, a little girl caught him,
All of a sudden, they blasted off,
And went zooming to Saturn,
The young girl, Jessica, got hungry,
So Fuzzy pulled out a picnic,
They started eating their cheese sandwiches,
When they disappeared!
They landed back on Earth,
Safe and sound,
Fuzzy started to float up,
Back to his cloud,
When he got there,
Someone was sitting on his cloud,
His name was Stuffy,
And now they are best friends.

Cleo Mckenna (10)
Phoenix Primary School, Liverpool

The Orange And Green Monster

Snake-like fangs and green eyes,
Orange and green skin,
He lived in a cave all alone in the dark,
He was really scary,
And had sharp claws and sharp teeth,
He sometimes got angry,
And he had three eyes,
The monster started scaring people in the street,
The people tried to fight it,
The monster hid under the bed,
It was silent, not violent,
The people looked everywhere,
And when they saw it, they grabbed it,
The monster ran away, back to its cave.

Charlie Paul O'Hagan (10)
Phoenix Primary School, Liverpool

Stich

My monster from under the bed,
Has a big fat head,
He has a lot of stitches,
From all his bumps and bruises.

During the night, he goes into the sky,
And has to fly high,
He has no friends,
And he hates bends.

He is wrinkly,
And has no pinky,
In the winter, he never wears hats,
And he pretends to be a bat.

Aimee-Lee Doughtery (10)
Phoenix Primary School, Liverpool

Confetti Yeti

Confetti Yeti was so adorable,
But she was so cheeky and bad,
She had a friend called Retsnom,
But she went back to her family on Mars,
She had a backpack with secret potions in it,
Confetti Yeti's favourite colour was purple,
Her favourite thing to eat was spaghetti,
She lived with her mum,
She could do a special thump with her powers,
She also lived with her dad and bad brother,
She went to the top of the snowy mountain,
To play with her brother Fangs.

Olivia Dolan (10)
Phoenix Primary School, Liverpool

Mr Cuddly

This monster is cute,
You may not think a monster can be cute,
But yes he is,
His name is Mr Cuddly,
He is cuddly,
He is always good and never bad,
He is always happy and never sad,
He has lots of hair,
He is very cute,
People love him.

Rhys Weir (10)
Phoenix Primary School, Liverpool

MONSTER POETRY - THE NORTH

Alphelia The Icy Monster

Alphelia was born in east Mexico,
She has a lot of friends (yes, ten friends!)
One called Charlie, another called Erica,
And we can't forget Izzy!
She is an icy monster (very icy indeed!)
She will win any contest (yes, nearly every contest!)
Alphelia is the top of her class!
She dreams about Shakespeare (oh, Alphelia!)
The icy hair of hers rarely needs a cut,
It is very heavy though,
So think twice before a trim!
Alphelia loves her life and it's nice, trust me!
She is five and loves her age,
And she should do while it lasts!

Jessica Service (8)
Plantation Primary School, Halewood

Bellatrix The Naughty Monster

Bellatrix is as creepy as a vampire,
She is as deadly as a great white shark,
She is as annoying as a child screaming,
She is a fluffy, scary monster.

Bellatrix is as clever as a teacher,
She is invisible like a ghost,
Her fangs are as sharp as a knife,
She is as short as me.

Bellatrix is as naughty as my little sister,
She is as pretty as my mum,
She is as skinny as a pencil.

Sophie Houghton (10)
Plantation Primary School, Halewood

The Truth

Monsters don't live under your bed
Why would they? Mars is far better
They live in school instead
Cunning as a fox, I got the monster letter

Staffrooms aren't just for eating cake
Teachers do something more exciting
I was going to find an oven to bake
But then I saw Miss Steady-Wrinkles baking

My teacher was just not herself
She was something far from that
Bright red horns, looking like an elf
It made the dancing trees stop dancing and lie on a mat

Mr Knight didn't know, but he was next!

Gracie Florence Scollen (10)
Robin Hood Primary School, Robin Hood

Dave

Deep deep down in a dark dingy cave,
There lived a monster, his name was Dave,
Dave was fierce, brave and bold,
But everyone thought he was mean and old.

Next to the cave there was a large icy lake,
Where children would play and learn to skate,
Dave would watch and wish he could join in,
But all of the children were scared of him.

The sun shone high, the ice wore thin,
One of the children fell right in!
The kids all screamed and got out of the lake,
All of the ice was about to break!

Dave saw the boy struggling to swim,
Within a second, Dave jumped in,
After splashing, wailing and flapping around,
A few seconds later, they were on solid ground.

The children gasped and stared at Dave,
He tried to turn and run back to his cave,
But the children shouted, "Stop!" and stood in Dave's way,

One of the children said, "Hey monster, do you want to play?"

Then Dave had friends and he really liked his cave,
All because of the boy he'd so bravely saved.

Daisy Lynch (7)
St Francis De Sales Catholic Junior School, Liverpool

Monster

The monster arrived suddenly,
Like a dark cloud, it hung around,
Making my heart pound and pound.

The trees trembled, the walls shook,
It wasn't your average monster from a bedtime book,
It happened so quickly, it happened so fast,
The rest of the family had to dash.

Brother, he went under the bed,
He had to be careful how he'd tread,
You needed to be careful, or you'd end up dead!

This monster was different,
Not a terrible beast,
Nor a zombie recently deceased,
Not a demon or the Devil himself,
Not even a scary 'Elf on the Shelf'!
Not anything like that!
He was like a normal man,
And here comes the twist...

The monster isn't under your bed,
If he finds you, you won't be dead,
It's not the guy with massive feet,
But it could be the strange guy lurking down the street!
Or it could be you, or even me!
It could be the man who drives the bus,
After all...

We've all got a monster inside of us!

Daniel Middlehurst (10)
St Francis De Sales Catholic Junior School, Liverpool

Prince Fang's Evil Plan

The darkest day you have ever seen,
Is where we begin our scene,
A monster jawed and roared,
Came closer and closer to my town,
Let's begin the story now.

It was a wacky Wednesday when we met,
And he caught me suddenly in his net,
Throwing me up and down,
Towards the ground,
Without a care in the world.

He took me to his cave,
And straight away began to call me Dave,
He told me his secret plan,
He also told me to call him Dan,
His plan was to take over the universe.

After he told me his name,
And he told me mine,
He sharpened his knife,
And he sharpened his fork,
I thought he was a bit of a dork!

Prince Fang was scary as could be,
And I'll tell you why,
Suddenly he put me on his plate,
Licking his lips as he stared at the plate,
Got his fork and knife ready, he really looked the part,
Stared at me intensely, then stabbed me in the heart!

Caitlyn Carragher-Leigh (8)
St Francis De Sales Catholic Junior School, Liverpool

Monster's Team

I had a dream,
The monster came to make me scream,
He was ugly, filthy and his name was Gream,
I asked Gream, "Why are you here?
Did you come to make me scream?"
Gream said, "I'm not here to make you scream,
I came here to get you on my team!"
I said, "I'm already on God's team
I don't want to be on your team!
At the moment, you are not welcome on God's team.
You have to make your heart clean,
And stop making children scream!
Love everyone, stop hating, be kind like a sunbeam,
And please stop appearing in everyone's dreams!"
Monster said, "If I do all this, will God put me on his team?"
I said, "God is lovely and so very kind,
His love always gleams,
So yes, he will take you on his team!"

After all of this, I could see the monster's eyes beam,
And I was also happy, as he never came back to my dream!

Muhammad Aashir (10)
St Francis De Sales Catholic Junior School, Liverpool

Funky Fin

There are lots of different monsters in this world,
There are monsters with wiggly arms and ones that are curled,
But my monster is different to all the other ones,
My monster is funky and always hums.

Now, I know what you are thinking,
What is this monster's name?
Well, my monster's name has gone down in fame,
This little monster is called Funky Fin,
And this furry monster lives in my bin.

He has big black eyes and a multicoloured Afro,
Plus his favourite food is mashed potato,
With his razor-sharp teeth, he may look scary,
But this cheeky monster is as sweet as a fairy.

Now let me tell you about Fin's fun night out,
Where he met a big, mean sprout!
He was out at the disco, having a great time,
When he met the furry, green sprout named Slime.

The evil monster said to poor Fin,
"I will eat you up, you little bin.
You do not belong in a place like here,
And you can barely listen with your ear!"
But Fin said back, "I don't care what you think!
After all, sprouts do stink!"

Well, that was the end of Fin's strange night,
Luckily, he didn't get in too much of a fight,
But there was one thing that Fin had learnt,
That it is good to stand up for yourself and be diverse!

Emily Forshaw (10)
St Francis De Sales Catholic Junior School, Liverpool

Brunzi And Me

Introducing... Brunzi,
My fairy, hairy monster,
With big blue eyes and purple hair,
She is caring and crazy, but clumsy.

Brunzi lives in my room,
To keep her out of trouble,
But once, she sneaked into my bag,
And my whole day went *boom!*

Firstly, when I was at school,
Brunzi knocked over the paint,
Leaving footprints all over the floor,
My teacher shouted, "Who is this fool?"

Then I went to my gymnastics session,
Brunzi joined in too,
Her forward rolls were very good,
But she needed a cartwheel lesson.

Finally, we got back home,
And I put Brunzi back in my room,
That day was a funny day,

And then Brunzi stole my phone!
Oh no!

Lexie Bruns (9)
St Francis De Sales Catholic Junior School, Liverpool

My Sneaky Neighbour

In the darkest of nights,
There lives a creature that causes fright,
But he's not as scary as you think,
His name is Omega,
As mysterious as the missing link.

Omega is tough,
He acts irresponsibly and is a bit of a scruff,
But not as scary as you think,
Omega is as mysterious as the missing link.

His two eyes are colossal,
But he never gives a smile,
And he lives alongside his wife and child,
Not lonely is little Omega,
His life is a living saga.

By day and night unseen,
He spreads his dragon wings and stays keen,
I know this about little Omega,
Because I am the one who is his neighbour.

Monsters are more scared of you,
Just like Omega, who's furry, soft and blue,
Now you know about my one-eyed friend,
He has red teeth and chubby pink wings, I don't pretend.

So if you see my naked, black-legged monster,
Do not engage!
Because if you do, he will release plasma with great rage.

Because in the darkest of nights,
There lives a dragon-like creature that causes fright,
But really, he's not as scary as you think,
And his name is Omega,
As mysterious as the missing link.

Joseph Collins (10)
St Francis De Sales Catholic Junior School, Liverpool

The Big-Eyed Monster

On my holiday,
I met a monster,
Not just any monster,
But a big-eyed monster,
That had enormous fangs!

He asked me to go somewhere I knew,
So I said that I would go,
There was no snow, but a big, bright glow,
Anything of this sort, he didn't know.

So when we got to the beach,
There were no seats,
There were a variety of drinks,
But unfortunately for him, there were no skating rinks!

Finally, when we went home,
We said goodbye to each other,
We were not going to Rome,
But we were leaving each other.

On my holiday,
I met a monster,
Not just any monster,
A big-eyed monster!

Jasmine Young (9)
St Francis De Sales Catholic Junior School, Liverpool

Monster Madness

Mum tucks me in and says goodnight,
Walks out of the room and turns off the light,
I lie in bed in the dark cold night,
Once again, I get a fright,
I hear a scratch,
I hear a squeak,
Is this night about to turn bleak?
"Roar!" cries the monster as it runs under my bed,
I fall right back and bump my head,
I see it shuffle out of my room,
I see the monster from the light of the moon,
It has light-coloured hair and is not that tall,
But it is very fast,
As it runs right past!
I step outside to see what's there,
Nothing at all but the dark, cold air,
"Back into bed, Tom!" I hear Mum say,
Does this monster just want to play?
I sit on my bed and feel quite scared,
But once again, the monster is there.
I jump right up and grab a little bin,

This is my chance to capture him!
The monster trips and falls over my shoes,
Stuck in the corner, it cannot move!
Yes, it has light-coloured hair and isn't that tall,
I finally realise it's not a monster at all!
With all the madness, this night has been crazy,
All along, it was my sister Daisy!

Tom Lynch (7)
St Francis De Sales Catholic Junior School, Liverpool

My Fearsome Frankey

There's a monster in my bedroom with a purple, fluffy head,
Sometimes he's in my wardrobe, sometimes he's in my bed,
I hear him moving in the dark, he likes to come out at night,
I've only seen him once or twice, he's not a pretty sight!
He has a big, fat, hairy tummy and teeth like a shark,
A tail that's four feet long and spots that glow in the dark.
One night I heard him moving, I screamed with all my might,
But the monster hid in the corner, so it was him who got a fright!
I turned the light on quickly so that I could see,
The monster sitting crying, he was just afraid of me!
I gave him a hug and now we are friends,
Of that I have no doubt,

If you see a monster, don't be scared,
It's what's inside that counts!

Niamh Ferguson (8)
St Francis De Sales Catholic Junior School, Liverpool

Not All Monsters Are Scary

Everything was dull and dark,
Until the appearance of my fluffy friend Mark,
Zem and Holly came along too,
Fluffy, blue-eyed and kind of smelling like poo!
The first time I met them, I felt like crying,
But the next day, they saved me from dying.

My story all began when,
I decided to make a pillow den,
I tossed and turned all night long,
But never slept at all because of Bong,
He is another monster of course, who is frightening and scary,
Did I mention he is also very hairy?
I couldn't sleep so I made a den,
But that's when it all happened again.

This monster arrived and tried to scare me,
But mysterious figures appeared - there were three,
Later on that day, I again saw them,
They were my fluffy friends, Mark, Holly and Zem.

Ever since that tragic day,
Our friendship has been more than okay,
I love them too, to the moon and back,
For Christmas, I even got them an Apple Mac!
The most important thing that I have learnt,
Is to keep your friends close because it's a
beautiful thing well earned.

Sienna McCready (11)
St Francis De Sales Catholic Junior School, Liverpool

The Snotrag Monster

There's a really grumpy monster,
Living under my bed,
His eyes are on stalks,
On the top of his head.

His hair is like a scarecrow's,
Sticking up in the air,
His teeth are all green,
And covered in fur!

He's got long, sharp nails,
For picking his nose,
Then he wipes off his bogies,
On my nice, clean clothes.

When he opens his mouth,
His breath really smells,
And he's never quiet,
He only ever yells!

This bad-tempered monster comes out every morning,
This monster is me when I wake up and I'm yawning.

Darren Herlihy (8)
St Francis De Sales Catholic Junior School, Liverpool

Fluffy Comes To School

I have a monster, his name is Fluffy,
And very fluffy he is,
Fluffy lives on my bed,
Once, he even climbed on my head!
One day, he jumped into my bag,
I told him that he had to go back,
But he locked himself in, so I could not see!
I got to school and opened up the zip,
I found him reading my book!
I told all my friends and I shouted, "Have a look!"
They laughed and gasped, they thought he was funny,
But my teacher caught me and said, "Who is he?"
I ran away with Fluffy, but I dropped him on the floor,
I panicked and panicked,
Until I found him swinging from the door,
We went home and had our tea,
Watched a movie and giggled with glee!

Caitlin Louise Kelly (10)
St Francis De Sales Catholic Junior School, Liverpool

The Hidden Monster

Once upon a time in a wood,
There was a monster that was not very good,
The terrified children let out their cries,
When they saw the monster and his five huge eyes!
They couldn't believe it was all just a dream,
Because of the sound of his bellowing scream!

He was spotty and scary,
And very, very hairy,
As he stomped on the ground,
You could hear a great sound,
He had lots of legs,
And his teeth looked like pegs!

The children all ran,
He was not looking for fun,
He could not catch them because they ran so fast,
So he hid in the trees, waiting for others to go past.

Ruby O'Brien (8)
St Francis De Sales Catholic Junior School, Liverpool

Monster Munch

My monster's name is Fiery,
He is so very hairy,
He has one eye,
That will make you cry,
And another two make him scary.

He wanders around at night,
And gives people a fright,
During the day, where does he stay?
Only I can say.

He lives in my world, under my bed,
And then, at night, he comes out in my head,
With his big, sharp teeth,
Searching for something to eat.

So stay away during the day,
Don't go for a munch,
Because you might end up,
Being Fiery's lunch!

Oliver Smith (8)
St Francis De Sales Catholic Junior School, Liverpool

The Monster Within The Monster's Skin

Too many eyes, too many legs,
Far too happy to be on my bed,
Loves to scare, but too scared to love,
He takes great pleasure at my frightened look,
But if you are so brave, why don't you face,
The terrifying truth within your heart?
The monster within the monster's skin.

Your furry back is filled with fleas,
Your toenails are ingrown and dirty,
Your belly is full and almost bursting,
But there is only one thing you should change,
The monster within the monster's skin.

I've heard you munching on the hidden packed lunch food,
In the wardrobe, behind an old pile of shoes,
Dad thinks it's us, but we know that it's you,
Mischief is your hobby; mayhem is your goal,
But when will you begin,
To deal with the monster in the monster's skin?

Evening arrives,
Light dims,
A quiet time to realise,
How wrong I was to demand of you,
When I have so much changing to do.

I look in the mirror... goodnight.

Elizabeth Doherty (11)
St Francis De Sales Catholic Junior School, Liverpool

Heartless

The name Flame Soul was all that it took to make you cower.
Its hypnotic deep black eyes were what drained you of your power.
The blood-curdling sight of it wasn't enough.
But the monster also had to be iniquitous and heartless, making you think it was better to give up.

The roaring of the monster invaded your ears,
While it was the sharp fangs inside its mouth that shook you to tears.
Bright yellow lightning bolts were the monster's signature mark,
Along with the fact that it was made up of flames - always scaring away the dark.

The monster was parentless, friendless and pure evil.
Which was a magnificent method for madness that was lethal.
Its horns were on top of its head like that of a devil.
With scars and cuts carving its head into several.

The monster's stomach was a dark pit hungry for souls.
And its thirst only quenched with your blood on its floors.

After all, the name Flame Soul was all that it took to make you cower.

Simra Nadim (10)
St Francis De Sales Catholic Junior School, Liverpool

What Are Monsters Really Like?

Monsters are usually hairy,
Some of them can be scary,
Some of them have lots of legs,
Some of them can make spiderwebs,
Monsters can have spots,
Some have lots!
Some monsters are round,
Some are loud.

My monster isn't like the others,
Unlike them, mine has many brothers,
My monster is pink and he is bright,
He brightens up my entire day and night,
My monster has eleven eyes,
Because he can see everything, he is very wise,
My monster, however, doesn't live under my bed,
Because my monster lives inside my head.

Kaysey Sherlock (11)
St Francis De Sales Catholic Junior School, Liverpool

The Good-Bad Monster

He wasn't scary,
He wasn't black or blue,
He was probably around six foot two,
His teeth were pointy like daggers,
And his fur was as thick as a badger's,
Eyes as bright as moonlight,
With huge, sharp teeth that could bite,
He went outside in the middle of the night,
And looked around for things to give a fight,
He went to see his mate,
Whose name was Nate,
He went into his house,
And saw a little running mouse,
He started to shout,
When no one was about,
I hope he will be back,
Will I see him again? I'll have to keep track.

Anthony Muren (9)
St Francis De Sales Catholic Junior School, Liverpool

Monster Mog

Crash went the window,
Bang went the door,
Then there was a hairy monster,
Lying on the floor.

Yelp went the children,
Startled was the dog,
Up stood the monster,
"Hello, my name is Mog!"

With big, grizzly hands,
And big, stomping feet,
He just wanted a cuddle,
The children were in for a treat.

Mog read them stories,
"Now off to your beds!
I'll give you a kiss goodnight,
Now rest your sleepy heads!"

Kaliah Nicholson (8)
St Francis De Sales Catholic Junior School, Liverpool

Oogie And Fang

There's a monster called Oogie,
And he really loves to boogie,
He comes from afar,
From a place called Mars,
His friend is called Fang,
And he makes a bang!
Together they act crazy,
For their little friend called Maisie,
They visit her at night,
And they try to give her a fright,
Fang makes a bang!
So Maisie starts to move,
But Oogie starts to boogie,
Then Maisie starts to groove,
After their dance, they all lie down to sleep,
And her mummy says, "Shh! I don't want to hear another peep!"

Maisie-Jane Perry (9)
St Francis De Sales Catholic Junior School, Liverpool

My Pet Monster

I have a pet monster,
His name is Ted,
He is rather large and furry,
And he lives under my bed.

He's got yellow teeth,
And big green spots,
He also likes to eat fish fingers and beans,
And the occasional moth!

He walks me to school, but no one sees him,
Are they blind?
"Don't be silly!" says my mum,
"The monster is in your mind!"

He sits at my desk and helps with my maths,
And when I go swimming, he cannonballs into the baths,
At night, whilst everyone's asleep, we sneak down to the fridge,
I eat all the strawberry yoghurts whilst Ted licks the lids.

Some people say Ted's not real,
And that my imagination has gone wild!
But Ted has always been with me,
Since I was a very small child.

I love my pet monster, he will always protect me,
I'm sure he'll sleep under my bed until I'm about twenty!

Lydia Katherine Quayle (8)
St Francis De Sales Catholic Junior School, Liverpool

Stinky Joe Destroys Liverpool

Once I met a monster called Stinky Joe,
Whose height was rather unbelievably low,
His entire body was covered in hair,
But his head was completely bare,
His tongue was long and stretchy,
He was kind of sketchy.

He always got into trouble,
Mostly for blowing bubbles,
His dream was to destroy Liverpool,
So he went there looking very cool.

He flew a helicopter in the sky,
And hoped the humans would say goodbye,
He landed his helicopter quickly in town,
So quickly, in fact, that the helicopter went very far down.

It went to the Earth's core,
A surprise to us all,

Stinky Joe became quite sad,
When he realised he had been very bad.

He came up with a plan,
And went to get a tree from Milan,
He stuffed it in the core far down below,
And everyone chanted, "Stinky Joe, you are our hero!"

Holly Louise Williams (9)
St Francis De Sales Catholic Junior School, Liverpool

The Merseyrail Monster

The Merseyrail Monster,
Is haunting these tracks,
It's been to Southport, Ormskirk, Kirkby and back,
If it heads to Southport,
It goes to the fair,
If it goes to Kirkby,
You'd better beware!
If it goes through the tunnel,
New Brighton is on watch,
It won't head to West Kirby,
That's far too posh!
Chester's an option,
But so is Hunt's Cross,
The monster's been to Lime Street,
It's still on the roam,
Will it end up in Bootle or maybe Old Roan?

Isabella Louise Blain (10)
St Francis De Sales Catholic Junior School, Liverpool

Monster Holiday

Whoosh!
Oh, goodbye Smoosh,
We've had so much fun,
But the time has inevitably come.

We will miss you and your rainbow eye,
That glistens like a star in the sky,
I will dearly miss your bright yellow fluff,
That reminds me of the monster on my box of Sugar Puffs!

You visited Liverpool,
And personally, I think it's cool,
You are going back to Mars,
Where there are flying cars,
I'm not going to cry,
After all, it's only a goodbye!

Lilly May Dunning (11)
St Francis De Sales Catholic Junior School, Liverpool

My Furry Friend

When I was sleeping in my bed,
On a dark and stormy night,
I heard a noise beneath my bed,
It gave me such a fright!

I opened up the cupboard door,
I thought I saw a face,
I peered inside and looked around,
It was just an empty space.

Then I heard some footsteps,
I turned around to see,
A blue and furry monster,
Staring back at me!

I put my arm around him,
And asked if he would stay,
He wasn't very scary,
He only wanted to play!

Lili Lou Tregunna (8)
St Francis De Sales Catholic Junior School, Liverpool

The Tar Monster

One day, when the tar was hot,
It started to bubble,
And up came the Tar Monster.

The monster was drooling,
The monster bubbled up,
He grabbed the children,
And strangled them.

The children were terrified,
Screaming for their lives,
The people in cars tried to escape,
But couldn't.

The Tar Monster, with its giant eyeball,
And black body as dark as midnight,
Ruled over the streets of London.

Neve Garvey (8)
St Francis De Sales Catholic Junior School, Liverpool

Flow's Day Out With Joe

There was a monster called Flow,
Everywhere she went, she played with her yo-yo,
Flow had a friend called Joe,
Who would glow when he was flying around in his UFO.

Flow would say hello,
And they would go and play in the snow,
Flow knew that she would glow,
Just like Joe in his UFO.

Joe, who was best friends with Flow,
Said, "Do you want a game of tic-tac-toe?"
"Sorry, but I've got to go!" said Flow,
So Joe replied by saying, "Next time you will glow!"

Krystal Natalie Sanders (9)
St Francis De Sales Catholic Junior School, Liverpool

Floating Death

In the sky, above your head,
You will say bye and be dead,
Snake head and hawk body,
Watch your back and don't move,
Death is near,
Listening out with your ear,
Floating death is here.

In Liverpool, on a sunny day,
We go to school on a bad day,
1.30pm, he is here,
Floating death is getting near,
We go outside, cowering in fear,
Someone has died, I drop a tear,
He is here, I shriek in fear,
Floating death is here.

Robert Chadwick Jr (11)
St Francis De Sales Catholic Junior School, Liverpool

My Monster

Some people have monsters that live under their bed,
Some live in wardrobes or even in people's heads,
Some are friendly, some are scary,
Some have six arms, some are hairy.

There are tall monsters and monsters that are small,
Some are loud and some are quiet and like to crawl,
Some have eyes that are really bright,
They can even light up the night.

However, my monster has a purple mermaid tail,
Also, the top half is a unicorn and is female,
She likes English and maths,
In class, there can't be any laughs,
Don't run! No fun!

Her teeth are sharp and ripe,
They could give you quite a fright,
Trying not to rest, hoping I'm the best,
Waiting for the results of my test,

As my friends and I have always said,
Teachers are aliens!
Gabriella Calder (10)
St Francis De Sales Catholic Junior School, Liverpool

Bill The Cleaning Monster

I know a monster, his name is Bill,
People think he's a statue because he stands so still.

Some people say he's scary and mean,
But not me, because Bill and I are a team.

He has sponges for feet and dusters for hands,
Bill just loves to clean up different lands.

Chores are never boring when Bill is around,
Because he sings and dances and makes funny sounds.

So when it's tidy up time and no one's about,
All I need to do is give my friend Bill a shout.

Daniel Connor (7)
St Francis De Sales Catholic Junior School, Liverpool

The Monster Who Loved To Dance

I had a monster who loved to dance,
Around the house he jumped and pranced,
Whilst rapidly the house would shake,
Until our precious vases would break!

He pointed his toe while in a tendu,
Whilst landing in a huge fondue!
His pink, fluffy fur which was as soft as a pillow,
Was no longer soft, cushioned or mellow!

I had a monster who loved to dance,
Around the house he jumped and pranced,
He danced every day and he danced every night,
And I danced with him, even though it gave him a fright!

Keira Harrison (10)
St Francis De Sales Catholic Junior School, Liverpool

The Mon'star'

I met a lovely monster,
Whose eyes were as bright as stars,
He said his name was Norman,
And his favourite thing was cars.

He wanted to be famous,
But he didn't have a plan,
So I asked him, "What are you good at?"
He replied, "Music is my jam!"

He jumped up to his feet,
And the room went *boom!*
Then he started to rap,
A melodic monster tune.

He had all the moves,
And a voice to impress,
It sure was a shame,
About his sense of dress!

I took out my phone,
And recorded his moves,

Suddenly my video,
Had thousands of views!

But nobody believed that he was real,
They thought it was a trick!
But I know him and he knows me,
And that's just the way it's got to be!

Isobel Moran (10)
St Francis De Sales Catholic Junior School, Liverpool

Monster From Mars

There is a monster called Zars,
Who has come from Mars,
To steal Earth's precious loot.

He can shape-shift into different sizes,
So don't blink with your eyes,
Or your phone or watch could be gone!

He'll steal the Crown Jewels,
And he owns five thousand pools,
Filled with hundreds and hundreds of pounds.

Although he's a chief,
He's called Monster Thief,
Because he has stolen your gold.

Layton James (8)
St Francis De Sales Catholic Junior School, Liverpool

The Hungry Monster

The greedy monster was such a hungry beast,
As soon as he woke up, he wanted a feast,
He would start the day with scrambled eggs and jumping frog's legs,
But still that wasn't enough,
For lunch he had nine steaks, he liked them super tough,
He never stopped eating,
To him it was fun,
For dinner he guzzled a giant burger in an even bigger bun,
Even before bed, he wanted lots more,
So he went out hunting and captured a wild boar,
Big, fat and juicy, it sure was a treat,
But even he couldn't eat its smelly feet.

Harry Shallcross (9)
St Francis De Sales Catholic Junior School, Liverpool

My New Friend

I met a furry creature,
Short and quite neat,
His name was Ozzie,
He came to my house and ate sweets,
He was fluffy like my teddy, Ted,
He was my new friend,
We went to the park and had a tea party,
He met my unicorn, Izzie,
Ozzie and I had a great day,
So he came back another day,
We went to the fair,
Came home and went upstairs,
To play with our new toys,
I love my new friend,
I hope he comes back soon.

Lexi Saunderson (9)
St Francis De Sales Catholic Junior School, Liverpool

Under The Bed

When night-time falls,
And everyone's asleep,
I hear footsteps about to creep,
Is it in the cupboard or under the stairs?
What's this I see? Is it something with hairs?
Shall I put on the light? I dare not move!
Is it a claw? Is it a hoof?
I hear a strange noise,
Scratching from down below,
It's starting to move,
This dark, dark shadow,
I hear a groan,
Like something wants to be fed,
I hear a voice say,
"Hello, I'm the monster from under your bed!"

Isabella May Bennett (11)
St Francis De Sales Catholic Junior School, Liverpool

There Are Different Types Of Monsters

Some monsters are red,
Some monsters are blue,
Some are quite cool,
Some act like a fool,
Some are quite talented,
Some can play pool,
Some are quite fast,
Some are quite slow,
Some glow green like a nightmare's dream,
Some monsters are lean,
Some monsters know the Queen,
Some act like Lightning McQueen,
Some have long limbs,
Some have funny-shaped hearts,
Some like even eating tarts!

Harley James Whittingham (10)
St Francis De Sales Catholic Junior School, Liverpool

Life Of The Monster Under Your Bed

Hi, my name is Claus the monster,
And I live under your bed,
I'm most happy when I'm being fed,
I have big ears and a big round head,
When you go to school, I sleep in your bed,
And I cuddle your teddy, whose name is Fred.

While you're at school, I wear your clothes,
I also play football and score lots of goals,
Before the end of the day, I get watered and fed,
And then I go to sleep under your bed,
With your ted, Fred.

Ella Harper (11)
St Francis De Sales Catholic Junior School, Liverpool

The Girl Whose Best Friend Was A Monster

As I do a pirouette, the only thing I see,
Is a big, fluffy monster sitting by the tree,
I ignore it, walk home and glance,
All of a sudden, the monster starts to do a funny dance.

I laugh and I chuckle like I do,
Because the monster says, "I have so much fun with you!"
We have the best time together,
Because we are the best of friends forever and ever.

My monster friend.

Jessica Sheridan (11)
St Francis De Sales Catholic Junior School, Liverpool

My Monster Friend

It was just an ordinary day,
So my monster and I went out to play,
Her name is Faye,
And mine is May.

We went down to the lake,
And we found a snake,
The lake was cold,
And we found it full of mould.

I found out it was moss,
So the day wasn't a loss,
"Goodbye!" I said,
"It was a wonderful day!"

Milly-Ann McDermott (9)
St Francis De Sales Catholic Junior School, Liverpool

The Monster In Your Dreams

He's got sharp teeth,
Big claws and huge jaws,
When you're asleep, he gives you a fright!
Then you wake up and it's still night,
When you're awake in the day, he's not there,
And you wonder why he's not giving you a scare,
As you get older, you realise he's not real,
He's just the monster in your dreams,
So really, there's no reason to scream!

Lizzie Cassin (8)
St Francis De Sales Catholic Junior School, Liverpool

The Mysterious Monster

I am brown, hairy and smelly,
I have big eyes and I'm very scary,
I hide behind the door all day long,
Waiting for a fly to come along,
Yum, yum, yum,
Dinner is all done,
The fly was nice,
But it would taste better with rice,
Now it is time to hide away,
Before the kids come home,
And I scare them away.

Thomas Morley-Healy (9)
St Francis De Sales Catholic Junior School, Liverpool

The Gentle Monster

Fluffy was born in a zoo,
But unlike all other animals,
She was a monster,
Fluffy, gentle, cute,
She escaped the zoo,
And went to Liverpool,
That's where I met this little blue monster.

As small as a mouse,
As cute as an arctic fox,
She ran around playing tag,
As gentle as one can be,
She was the prettiest monster I ever did see.

We went shopping and I bought some things,
Chocolate, marshmallow and jelly rings,
Just enough for a royal feast,
For me and my mini beast.

Isabelle Louisa Edwards (10)
St Francis De Sales Catholic Junior School, Liverpool

Where Monster Live

Smelly socks, sweet wrappers and books,
Lying discarded under the bed,
Forgotten forever by those who do not want to remember,
But a collection for something or someone,
In the dead of night instead,
Lurking and waiting for silence to begin,
The creeping and scaring will make you jump out of your skin,
Move if you dare!
Open your eyes,
I promise you, there will be no surprise,
From under your bed, whilst you're lost in your dreams,
His favourite moment of all is listening to your screams!

Rae Hynds (10)
St Francis De Sales Catholic Junior School, Liverpool

The Big Blue Lonely Monster

In my nan's back garden,
Lives a monster big and blue,
He is a lovely monster,
I promise you it's true.

He doesn't scare us children,
Despite the way he looks,
He always has a barbecue,
And he's the one who cooks!

He teaches us new tricks,
Almost every single day,
He makes us very happy,
When we go out to play.

I love my big blue monster,
I really, really do,
I love my big blue monster,
His name is Balou.

Scarlett Conlan (7)
St Francis De Sales Catholic Junior School, Liverpool

The Hairy Man Friend

There was a big, brown monster that was tall and hairy,
When all the kids saw him, they thought he was scary,
No one knew that he was good,
Except this one boy who played in the neighbourhood,
But then, one day, his loneliness came to an end,
And he became everyone's friend.

Alfie Walsh (9)
St Francis De Sales Catholic Junior School, Liverpool

My Monster And Me!

One day, I was on a bike ride,
Then suddenly, I got a big surprise,
A huge, fluffy monster I could see,
Standing behind me, staring at me,
Next to it was a big, bubbly monster.

My beautiful cheeky Charlotte,
Didn't have any friends,
Except from that one special friend,
The monster called Rachet,
Rachet was her only best friend.

Me, my monster and Rachet,
Went to the pet shop,
And I said, "Oi! That's my monster!"
As the evil shopkeeper took her away.

My heart broke as I saw her crying face,
"Come back!" I shouted,
I ran after her like I was in a race,
It was a disgrace.

Ava Roberts (9)
St Joseph's Washington RC School, Washington

MONSTER POETRY - THE NORTH

Eye Ball Ed

My monster's name is Ed,
And he has a friend called Fred,
He is as soft as a bunny and likes to lick honey,
He comes from a monster water park,
That has a towering 100,000 foot slide!

He took me to the water park,
Where everyone likes to play,
But when the children saw him,
They screamed and ran away.

My monster took me on the bright blue 100,000 foot slide,
We felt our legs wobbling and our heads shaking,
It was the most jaw-dropping ride ever!

We ran over to the next ride,
And he saw his friend called Fred,
After the ride, we had to go home,
But it was the best day ever!

Katie Muir (9)
St Joseph's Washington RC School, Washington

Monsters Are Not That Bad

I found my monster at the park,
He had a great smile from the start,
We said hi on the count of three,
Maybe we had the key to fun,
"Fun! Fun!" that's what he said,
With his cute eyes like buttons.

We went to the moon in a hot air balloon,
He was about six foot two,
And then he told me his name was Hairy,
Hairy Harry,
And suddenly, we went down, down, down.

After, we had a picnic,
A picnic with some tea and a scone,
Soon it was time to go,
But he said, "Don't cry! After all,
Monsters are not that bad!"

Eva Alexandra Smith (9)
St Joseph's Washington RC School, Washington

The Cute Friendly Monster

My monster's name is Friendly Phoebe,
She has a friend called Bob,
She likes to run around with him and eat lollipops,
When we go to the fair,
She always wants to get a giant teddy bear,
Phoebe has teeth that are as white as a ghost,
She is hairy and purple and has a horn like a unicorn,
I took her to school and all my friends said she was cool,
Me and my monster went to the shop,
She said she wanted a top that said, 'Lollipop!',
We finally went home,
I said that we'd had a great adventure,
Phoebe said, "Can we go to the moon, moon, moon?"
I said, "Maybe tomorrow, tomorrow, tomorrow!"

Misia Ograbek (10)
St Joseph's Washington RC School, Washington

Fluffy The Mosnter

It was a rainy night,
And people were having a fight,
There was a bang in the sky,
I didn't want to cry,
There was a hole in the ground,
And a flap opened,
It was a monster called Fluffy!

He had lost his wig,
He said, "It looks like a twig."
We went to a water park,
Where it was dark,
He jumped in the pool,
It was very cool,
It was way better than school,
The next day he sent me a letter,
Saying that I could visit.

Taylor Paul Jacklin (9)
St Joseph's Washington RC School, Washington

The Monster Under The Bed

I woke up and looked under the bed with one eye,
I looked and it was a monster,
I turned around and touched the ground,
He was still there,
I couldn't believe my eyes,
He looked slim and had scales,
Although he was kind of frail,
I named him Scary Sid,
I took him to a Newcastle match,
Which he didn't really like,
He tried to eat the ball,
And got me kicked out of the match,
He won't be doing that again!

Lennon Jay Liddle (9)
St Joseph's Washington RC School, Washington

Cutie, Not A Beast

My monster's name is Fred,
He has a friend called Ed,
He is as soft as a bear,
And he sits in your hair.

He comes from a monster water park,
With 100,000 foot tall slides,
And if you try to tickle him,
He runs away and hides.

He took me to the water park,
Where everyone likes to play,
But when the children saw him,
They screamed and ran away.

He took me to the bright blue slide,
And eventually, when I got to the top,
I went down and landed in the pool with a plop!

On the way home, I went to the shop,
To buy some slop for my monster,
He said to me, "Goodbye,
And I swear I will not lie.

I'll see you sometime,
By the way, my favourite food is limes."

Katie Robinson (9)
St Joseph's Washington RC School, Washington

Me And My Monster

Two days ago, I was in my car,
Suddenly, I saw a happy, short monster,
I went to the shop,
The monster's jaw began to drop,
He said, "Hello! My name is Ozzy!
I come from Planet Valerian.
I am a fuzzy monster.
I like to buzz around,
I like to jump on the ground."
We went to the park,
And he said he wanted a lollipop.

Sonny Evin Liddle (9)
St Joseph's Washington RC School, Washington

Hairy Harry

One day, I was walking to the park,
When I saw a big spark,
It was a horrible, hairy creature,
And then he said, "Nice to meet you."

A while later, he started to frown,
But then I said, "Why are you wearing a crown?"
Then I said, "What's your name?"
He said, "Hairy Harry."

He was nearly all blue,
And he was about six foot two,
I said, "Where do you come from?"
He said, "Far, far, far away."

Alfie Joe Wilson (9)
St Joseph's Washington RC School, Washington

My Friend

I had a monster called Four-Legged Bob,
His favourite place was the funfair,
All he wanted was a big teddy bear,
He wanted the one that looked just like,
His best friend, Friendly Phoebe,
He turned around and there she was,
Eating French fries from a box,
Bob tried, tried and tried again,
Until he got it,
He shouted, "I've got it! I've got it!"
We went on a couple more rides,
Then I went home,
And Bob went to Mars.

Emily Richardson (9)
St Joseph's Washington RC School, Washington

Fame Lover

On the way to the park,
I met a monster in the dark,
He told me his name,
Which was Neon Craine,
He had a bright orange body,
And bright blue legs,
Which were oozy and slippery,
He had come to Earth to find worldwide fame!
He followed me home,
And pinched my dog's bone!
I told him, "No! Bad boy! Leave it alone!"
And then I got him his own,
He asked if he could play,
But I told him, "Not today!"
Suddenly, he looked all glum,
I said, "What's up? Should I call your mum?"
The monster shook his head,
It was time for his bed.

Niall Bruce (8)
St Patrick's RC Primary School, Ryhope

Murphee The Monster!

On the way to the park I met,
A monster who had four eyes and was blue,
He asked if we could go to London,
To visit his friend in the dungeon,
"Of course!" I said,
"Woohoo!" he said,
As he slithered off to bed.

The next morning, he woke up,
With a gigantic hiccup,
He wanted his friends to come,
I asked who they were,
He said they were called Bop, Miggle and Nop,
"Yeah, fine, let's go!" I replied.

In a flash, we were there,
I shouted up the tower, "Miggle, let down your hair!
Okay now, let's go to the royal wedding."
"No not yet, we still need to get Bop and Nop!"
"Where are they?" I asked,
"They are at the London Eye," he answered.

We rushed there and picked them up,
Then we were off to the royal wedding,
To see Prince Harry and Princess Meghan.

The bride wore a beautiful white dress which was flowing,
She looked gorgeous, you could even say she was glowing,
Prince Harry stood at the bottom of the aisle looking very smart,
He had on his military uniform and certainly looked the part!

The day came to an end,
But at least I'd made some new friends!

Hannah Naisbitt (9)
St Patrick's RC Primary School, Ryhope

The Walk From Space

On the way to Earth I met,
A monster giving birth,
Out popped a purple Smurf,
It bounced onto a monster called Boodoo,
Who started to cry, "Boohoo!"
Boodoo fell over,
He got back up like nothing had happened.

Suddenly, he found a lucky four-leaf clover,
The clover looked like a delicious, tasty brick,
So the blue-haired monster took a lick,
It tasted like a burger,
So Boodoo said, "I might take a bite."

But before he did,
He got hit in the eye by a mighty kite!
The kite was as red as blood,
It had brown lines as dark as mud.

There was a monster in town,
It had an unpleasant frown,
Boodoo smelt his breath,
"Goodness me!" Boodoo said, "You've got bad breath!"

Boodoo couldn't save the Earth,
So he flew back to Migglepop,
To adopt a Smurf.

Zanyar Mohammed (9)
St Patrick's RC Primary School, Ryhope

Cuddly Puff's Adventure In France

On the way to France I met,
A monster cute and cuddly,
She was hiding from me in a dumpster,
So she was very wet,
I got a cloth and dried her off.

She said she was from Planet Blub-Blub,
It was a lovely planet full of love,
I asked her where her planet was,
She replied, "Near Planet Nub-Nub,
Where all they do is shove."

We started our adventure in France,
And she said, "My name is Cuddly Puff and I love friends."
I asked her what their names were,
She replied, "Fluff But and Fuzzy Nut,
And our friendship will never end."

I showed her the Eiffel Tower,
And she said, "That looks like Fuzzy Fred."

I replied, "Who is he?"
And she said, "He's my friend, but the monster I miss most,
Is little baby Ed."

We began to walk again and we smelt some lovely pastries,
Suddenly, the heart on her tummy began to glow,
I asked her what it meant,
And she said, "It means I have to go!"

Hannah Neal (10)
St Patrick's RC Primary School, Ryhope

Fluffy The Yeti

On the way to school,
Out of the blue,
Came a big, ecstatic yeti!

He had claws as sharp as razor blades,
And fur as soft as a pillow,
When he spoke, he sounded like an armadillo.

It was a school day,
So I had to take him with me,
It was good,
It was bring your pet to school day.

The next day, it was my birthday,
So my mum took me to Smiggle,
I tickled Fluffy with a soft pen,
He giggled so hard when he sneezed,
The shopkeeper flew over his knees.

Ruby Clark (9)
St Patrick's RC Primary School, Ryhope

A Strange Friend Chip!

On the way to school I met,
A green and blue monster who had brought his pet,
Both of us went into class,
Then I realised we had to go to Mass,
Halfway through, he burped in front of everyone,
I was really embarrassed (it was not something I would've done),
When we got back, it was lunchtime,
He had a plate full of chips only,
When Mr Hauxwell finished trying to teach,
Me and my friend went to the beach,
The waves were towering, scary and high,
And I thought to myself with a gulp, *we're going to die!*
But the monster (Earth Jr) was not scared at all,
He'd been surfing before and knew it all,
He looked at me kindly and said with a smile,
"Don't worry, Theo, I'll help you get by."
Every since that day, our friendship persists,
And the funniest thing is, we both love chips.

Theo Anthony Price (9)
St Patrick's RC Primary School, Ryhope

Spider Scar Nightmare

On the way to the cinema I met,
A monster saying he wanted me as a pet,
As he was taking over my town,
Blood from his mouth came oozing down,
He killed people with his sharp wings and knife of death,
He watched everyone he killed take one last breath,
He was as strong as a giant,
He told me his name was Spider Scar,
He hated the loud noise of alarms,
And tried to stay calm,
He was vicious and violent,
Then everything turned silent,
He could make your spine tingle,
Ever since he's been alive he's been single,
Spider Scar is treacherous and loves a jingle.

Abrahim Ahmed Umar (9)
St Patrick's RC Primary School, Ryhope

Hornacorn!

On the way to school,
I went to put my rubbish in the bin,
Then I found a monster in a dumpster,
With a face that was blue,
He was about six foot two,
There was something special about him,
He had a horn on his head,
And his name was Fred,
He asked to go on a trip,
As he was desperate to go on a cruise ship,
We went to France to visit the Eiffel Tower,
Which he tried to devour,
We left in a hurry,
I said, "Instead, why don't we get a curry?"

Millie Wake (10)
St Patrick's RC Primary School, Ryhope

Pip The Myth

In the park I met,
A monster who was hiding in the dark,
His name was Pip,
And he was a myth,
He had four arms!
I asked him, "How old are you?"
He replied, "I am two and made of glue."
We went to school,
And we went in the pool,
After school, we saw a fluffy puppy,
Pip scared the puppy,
Then he turned pink and blue,
Which meant he had to go,
We went back to the park,
Sadly, Pip went back into the dark.

Nathan Jones (9)
St Patrick's RC Primary School, Ryhope

The Green Monster

On the way to the park I met,
A monster who was green, slimy and wet,
He decided to go and sit,
And just watch the running kids who were very fit.

He loved to eat rice,
"Yum!" he'd say. "It tastes nice!"
He went into a busy town,
He walked around and around.

The people all stopped and stared,
His deep blue eyes rolled around in his head,
He didn't like the noise in the town,
So he went back to play with his two friends.

Owen Hunt (10)
St Patrick's RC Primary School, Ryhope

School Day With My Pet

On the way to school I met,
A kind monster in a pool,
He jumped out and followed me all the way,
So, politely, I asked him to stay,
We hurried to the classroom,
But sadly, there were no chairs,
So me and my monster sat on the stairs,
The lesson was history,
After five minutes, the monster said,
"Tutankhamun, that's a mystery!"
Then the bell rang,
During break we sang,
The day went by and before we knew it,
It was time to say goodbye.

Jessica Hartnett (9)
St Patrick's RC Primary School, Ryhope

Bubble Trouble

My monster is called Bubbles,
He doesn't make too much trouble,
He has blue eyes which glow in the night,
And he always thinks he's right.

He regularly stays in his socks,
And has a frightening picture of a fox,
The monster is so funny,
He doesn't realise he's a dummy.

He tried to scare the kids one night,
I told my friends, "He doesn't bite."
We tickled him to have some fun,
He got upset and started to run.

We watched him disappear into the dark,
The next day, we found him in the park,
My monster who is fluffy and blue,
He is about four foot two.

He's my friend, I love him to bits,
Even when he has got giant hair nits!

Maha Fazal Umar (10)
St Patrick's RC Primary School, Ryhope

Aphmau's Breadstick Adventure

On the way to Olive Garden I met,
Aphmau, a very orange monster,
I said, "Do you like breadsticks?"
She replied, "No, my favourite is red bricks!"

She was fluffy and kawaii,
She told me her birthday was in July,
Suddenly, we heard a subtle scream,
"What's that? It sounds mean!"

We ran to see what was wrong,
It was the evil sour breadstick, Mr Bitter Butter,
Aphmau bit his foot and then blew him up,
He yelled, "That's my butt!"

Aphmau thought it was a bit extreme,
And I bellowed, "That's enough!"
We both left in a hurry,
It was six o'clock and time for her red brick curry!

Lilly Jane Sillett (9)
St Patrick's RC Primary School, Ryhope

Monster Holiday

One day, whilst flying over Spain,
I spotted a monster on my plane,
"A monster?" I hear you say,
Yes, even monsters go on holiday,
I went over and said, "Hi!"
And he looked back with his fourth eye,
I asked him his name,
He said, "Mr 4, can you guess why?"
"No," which was a lie,
Because it was clear for all to see,
He had four of everything, even knees!
Now, Mr 4 did smell sweet,
A lot like a doughnut, good enough to eat,
As the plane came in to land,
Mr 4 asked if I would hold his hand,
In Spain we did arrive,
Me and Mr 4 did a big high five,
Although I say five, for him it was a low four.

Daniel Baines (9)
St Patrick's RC Primary School, Ryhope

The Chocolate Factory

My name is Clever Kevin,
And I live at number seven,
I come from Mars,
And own lots of cars,
I'm a good monster,
With a friend called Chompster,
We go to the chocolate factory every other day,
Eating lots of Mars bars on the way,
Once we have eaten all the chocolate there,
It makes us look like Care Bears!
The chocolate factory is brill,
We always hope it won't make us ill!

Jensen Andrew Howe (9)
St Patrick's RC Primary School, Ryhope

Bing Bang Boo

The monster who came out to play,
I really wanted her to stay,
Her name was Bing Bang Boo,
She came from the planet 072,
She was small, cute and fluffy,
We went to the park to get scruffy,
At home we played in the toy room,
There she drank my perfume,
At tea her fur turned blue,
As she ate too much glue,
In the middle of the night she went home,
I miss my Bing Bang Boo.

Harriet Westoe (9)
St Patrick's RC Primary School, Ryhope

Monster Friend

On the way to the playground I met,
A cute, shiny monster I'd like as a pet,
She was gentle and kind,
The best friend I'd ever find,
Her skin was light brown,
She had a slight frown,
I gave her a huge cuddle,
Which felt like a warm snuggle,
I could smell delicious cookies and cream,
So we went to look for some ice cream
We were so excited on the way,
We found the swings and started to play,
There was laughter and giggles everywhere,
The sound of happiness filled the air,
The day was nearly over,
Then she waved and said, "Bye, see you tomorrow."

Jessica Lei Howe (9)
St Patrick's RC Primary School, Ryhope

The Monster From Zabale

I met a monster on my way to school,
He growled at me, I felt a fool,
My legs, they wobbled and wobbled,
Would he eat me in one gobble?
He lived in a dirty, dark hole,
On the planet called Zabole,
I took him to lunch at KFC,
To eat some chicken instead of me,
His teeth were yellow and sharp,
His skin was black and blue,
You couldn't see him in the dark.

Maddie Stoodley (10)
St Patrick's RC Primary School, Ryhope

Burrito Madness

On the way to school I met a monster,
Who had muscles as big as his dad's,
But it was a shame his behaviour was really bad,
When we arrived at school,
Pupils said he was scary,
As he was extremely hairy,
His favourite food was a burrito,
And his favourite song was 'Despacito',
He liked to play tennis,
With his little brother Dennis,
As the school day came to an end,
He said goodbye to his teacher who he drove round the bend!

Jack Slee (9)
St Patrick's RC Primary School, Ryhope

MONSTER POETRY - THE NORTH

Fernkins The Monster

I met a monster on my way to school,
I thought he was sitting on a stool,
He stood up and I saw,
It was his friend on the floor,
He said his name was Fernkins,
His friend was called Bernkins,
Bleep blop, bleep blop, went his flying saucer,
He said it needed fizzy water,
His skin was golden-yellow,
And he was a lovely fellow,
He really was a nice guy,
His favourite food was chicken pie.

Michael Henry Hackett (10)
St Patrick's RC Primary School, Ryhope

Fluffy The Monster

He's a crazy chatterbox,
Not a flying, smelly fox,
White and blue,
He's coming to get you.

His name is Fluffy,
He's very, very puffy,
He doesn't like to have a shower,
But he has a lot of power.

He's spotty on his head,
And dotty on his legs,
He has a pretty kitty,
A very pretty kitty.

Cries like a baby,
But isn't afraid of gravy,
He's got a pretty big mouth,
But doesn't go down south.

Chloe Grace Greenwood (9)
Stoneferry Primary School, Hull

My Monster

My monster is small,
But that isn't all.

My monster is cheeky,
But is never freaky.

My monster likes to play,
But not all day.

My monster makes a lot of noise,
He even screams at his toys.

My monster creates a bad smell,
And doesn't hide it very well.

My monster always eats,
He never says no to treats.

My monster always makes a mess,
It's getting more often, rather than less.

My monster needs lots of sleep,
When he's tired, he collapses in a heap.

My monster is surprisingly fast,
But it doesn't last.

My monster is extremely cute,
But completely dislikes fruit.

My monster makes me proud,
Even if he's a bit too loud.

Charlotte Olivia Hawkin (10)
Three Lane Ends Academy, Castleford

Byron's Day At School

There is a monster in my school,
I think he is pretty cool,
He is as fluffy as a lion,
All the children call him Byron,
Six squirmy arms, long and blue,
Wave at the children dancing through,
Caterpillar fingers and smooth pink nails,
Cling onto storybooks and fairy tales,
Big, round eyes that glow like the moon,
Smiling brightly while he whistles a tune,
Perched by his feet is his pet cat,
Green and spiky and wearing a hat,
After lunchtime in the hall,
The pair join the children playing with a ball,
They giggle and laugh with their friends,
Hoping this fun day never ends,
But the school bell rings and it's time to go,
He knows he'll see them tomorrow,
Now the day is finally done,
He'll dream about tomorrow's fun!

Keira Marshall (10)
Wargrave CE Primary School, Newton-Le-Willows

The Funky Grunky

The Funky Grunky was mean and bad,
As mean and bad as your history teacher,
He lived all alone in a cave on a hill,
And was the grouchiest of all creatures.

One day, he decided to go to town,
And cause some mischief,
In town he met,
A small, little boy named Pete.

At first, Pete was very scared,
And began to run away,
But, as he turned, his headphones fell out,
And music started to play.

The Funky Grunky's burnt black skin,
Began to shine and shimmer,
His dull grey eyes were glowing green,
And soon began to glimmer.

Then he started to groove,
And twirl and twist and whoosh,

He spun around and leapt up high,
This monster had some moves.

Now, you see, the Funky Grunky wasn't all that bad,
He was just lonely and very, very sad.

Zahra Bhatti (9)
Wargrave CE Primary School, Newton-Le-Willows

Monster Fright At The Fairground

Bob was born in the deep depths of the sea,
He was a pirate monster who was really mean,
He had a red bloodshot eye with golden teeth and tattoos,
He had one leg and pale blue skin covering his six pack,
He had horns on the top of his head as red as a rose.

He had two idiotic friends called Jeff and Mike,
Who loved nothing more than to give you a fright,
They hung around the creepy fair,
And gave everyone who entered a really big scare.

Then one day, a young boy called Sid,
Came to the fairground and this is what he did,
As quick as a flash, the three monsters appeared,
They tried to spook him with a growl and a jeer.

But no, Sid just laughed, he didn't scream,
He didn't run, he didn't quiver,

So the three monsters started to shiver.

In disgust, Bob, Mike and Jeff ran away from the fairground,
And they haven't been seen to this day.

George Cain-Morris (9)
Wargrave CE Primary School, Newton-Le-Willows

Why Is It Always Me?

Why is it always me?
I climbed up a tree to get apples for my tea,
But on my way down, I got stung by a bumblebee.

Why is it always me?
I looked over the side of a boat,
But I fell straight into the sea.

Why is it always me?
I was eating my pudding while watching Bugs Bunny,
But my mum scared me so I dropped custard on my belly.

Why is it always me?
So all my friends now call me Clumsy Custard,
Guess that's better than Mucky Mustard.

I live in a small town called Jiggly Jelly,
It's perfect for me with my big, fluffy belly.

Why is it always me?
At the end of the day when I'm in bed,

Why do I always trip and bang my head?

Please tell me, why is it always me?

Lucy Lee (10)
Wargrave CE Primary School, Newton-Le-Willows

Fluffy The Monster

When I was in my bed,
Thoughts and sounds swirled around my head,
Not knowing what to do,
I jumped up to find a clue.

I looked behind the curtains and then under my bed,
Next it was my wardrobe, which really was a mess!
And there it was, something pink and fluffy with massive, sparkly eyes,
I ran from it as fast as I could due to my surprise.

I paused and thought I could be wrong about the furry monster,
So I turned and crept back up the stairs to take another gander,
I couldn't believe how sad it looked and that it'd made me run away,
All this monster wanted to do was hug, dance and play.

Now we are the best of friends,
We laugh and smile all day,
Life is so much fun now Fluffy's come to stay!

Alyssa Pritchard (9)
Wargrave CE Primary School, Newton-Le-Willows

The Midnight Fury

The Midnight Fury lives in outer space,
She has shining, purple eyes that light up her face,
She's as tall as a giant and flies very fast,
She's even overtaken a rocket in the past!

Glowing in the dark is her special power,
She guides astronauts with her light hour after hour,
For a dragon, she's kind and as wise as an owl,
But most people assume that dragons are foul.

Her friends are all good dragons like her,
They look after each other and always share,
They fly around the galaxies and love to play,
But even dragons get tired at the end of the day.

The midnight moon is where she sleeps and rests,
Out of all the dragons in outer space,
She's definitely the best!

Talia Grace Moorhouse (9)
Wargrave CE Primary School, Newton-Le-Willows

Scary Hugs

Heads, he has two,
Gives him the best view,
He's coming for you.

With his razor-sharp teeth,
And four eyes beneath,
He's coming for you.

His eyes of blue,
Are staring at you,
He's coming for you.

His giant, furry legs,
As thin as pegs,
He's coming for you.

The claws on his feet,
You don't want to meet,
He's coming for you.

He's coming for you,
He only eats bugs,
He's coming for you,
To give you the biggest of hugs!

Sophie Littler (9)
Wargrave CE Primary School, Newton-Le-Willows

Bad And Good Land

There was a monster called Mojo,
She was from the land of Dojo,
She had a friend called Coocoo,
She was from the world called Booboo.

One day, they went for a walk,
And they had a talk,
They saw Hunter who had a big mouth,
And always told a lie,
They just ignored him and went for a pie.

Nobody likes people who tell lies,
So that's why they walked on by,
Hunter apologised for the lies he'd told,
He gave them each a flower to hold.

They hugged him, they laughed and they walked,
They went for a swim,
Then they were the best of friends.

Francesca Hadaway (8)
Wargrave CE Primary School, Newton-Le-Willows

The Gingerninja

The Gingerninja of the Planet Gorinja,
Was born in an oasis of ginger.

The Gingerninja of the Planet Gorinja,
Is good at pranks but not a singer.

He is spiky and orange with antennae on his head,
His pranks are so funny, you might end up dead.

He is mischievous but cheerful,
His cyborg arm makes people quite fearful.

He has lots of friends, maybe millions,
He plays lots of pranks, billions and trillions.

He wears sunglasses on his face,
The Prankorium is his most favourite place.

When he pranks, nobody is safe,
His special itching powder will make you chafe.

You may wonder why I know so,
There's something that you all should know...

I am the Gingerninja of the Planet Gorinja!

Corbin Holmes (8)
Wargrave CE Primary School, Newton-Le-Willows

The Golden Flare

The Golden Flare is very rare indeed,
He lives in a volcano full of lava,
And causes such a palaver.

He is awfully awful and bad-mannered,
With big blue eyes that glow,
He loves to make chaos,
With horns as sharp as a blade.

He smells like a breath of fresh air,
And lives in a town called Bel-Air,
When the rain eases, he gets quite happy,
With a heart full of joy and happiness.

He's been left in the volcano,
To adventure all alone,
His tail is quite fluffy,
He's got a big mouth,
And a fire burns in his heart of desire.

Sometimes he makes people sad,
But mostly glad,
With the tip of his horn,

He tried to poke me once,
But I said, "Go away, fiery breath!"
And he disappeared in mid-air.

Chloe Grace Edwards (8)
Wargrave CE Primary School, Newton-Le-Willows

Muto's Family Adventure

There once was a monster called Muto,
Who came from a planet called Pluto,
She was fluffy and pink,
She let off a stink,
But some said she was still cute though.

Muto had a sister called Loo Loo,
Who whinged and cried, "Boohoo!"
She was ugly and bumpy,
She was loud and she was jumpy,
She never stopped shouting, "Yoo hoo!"

So Muto and Loo Loo loved dancing,
If they were not singing, they were prancing,
With their tutus and bows,
And big, hairy toes,
Anyone would've thought they were romancing.

Loo Loo and Muto's dad thought they were crazy,
But that beat them being lazy,
They were doing no harm,
There was no need to be calm,
Their mum was called Big Daisy.

Aleisha Gorman (9)
Wargrave CE Primary School, Newton-Le-Willows

The Cat Of Doom

My werecat's name is Gingey,
He prowls the house at night,
When he sees the family,
He gives them such a fright.

By day, he is small and ginger,
He is quite a normal cat,
But when the clock strikes midnight,
He puts on his monster hat.

He thinks he is big and scary,
With his little fangs and claws,
But in reality, he's just quite daft and cute,
He stalks Pipit Avenue looking for some loot.

Euan Stephen Arthur Adams (10)
Wargrave CE Primary School, Newton-Le-Willows

Hacry Hugglemonster

Hacry was born in Holzer Town,
He never smiles but always frowns,
Hacry is so smart that he farts,
Maths sums out of his bum,
Now, there's a boy called Hory,
Who's very mean and never cleans,
He calls Hacry nerdy,
And then flies off like a birdy,
Hacry used to be very lonely,
But then he met a friend,
His friend can bend, bend, bend!

Hayden Davis (10)
Wargrave CE Primary School, Newton-Le-Willows

The Monster Looney Uni

My friend is a monster unicorn,
She has a great big spotty horn,
When I go up to get into bed,
Looney Uni jumps on my head!

When I wake up the very next day,
Looney Uni says, "Do you want to play?"
I say, "Yes, as you are the best!"
Then Looney Uni shouts, "Hip hip hooray!"

So off we go to the woods to play,
To roll around in the grass and hay,
We have so much fun playing in the sun,
Then Looney Uni flies away!

Erin Elyse Crossland (8)
Wargrave CE Primary School, Newton-Le-Willows

YOUNG WRITERS INFORMATION

We hope you have enjoyed reading this book – and that you will continue to in the coming years.

If you're a young writer who enjoys reading and creative writing, or the parent of an enthusiastic poet or story writer, do visit our website **www.youngwriters.co.uk**. Here you will find free competitions, workshops and games, as well as recommended reads, a poetry glossary and our blog.

If you would like to order further copies of this book, or any of our other titles, then please give us a call or visit **www.youngwriters.co.uk**.

Young Writers
Remus House
Coltsfoot Drive
Peterborough
PE2 9BF
(01733) 890066
info@youngwriters.co.uk